Howard Zinn
on War

hello

Howard Zinn on War

Howard Zinn

SEVEN STORIES PRESS
New York • London • Sydney • Toronto

Copyright © 2001 by Howard Zinn

A Seven Stories Press First Edition

Some of the material in this book appears in *The Zinn Reader* (Seven Stories Press, 1997).

Seven Stories Press
140 Watts Street
New York, NY 10013
www.sevenstories.com

In Canada:
Hushion House, 36 Northline Road, Toronto, Ontario M4B 3E2

In the U.K.:
Turnaround Publisher Services Ltd., Unit 3, Olympia Trading Estate, Coburg Road, Wood Green, London N22 6TZ

In Australia: Tower Books, 9/19 Rodborough Road, Frenchs Forest NSW 2086

Library of Congress Cataloging-in-Publication Data

Zinn, Howard, 1922–
Howard Zinn on war / Howard Zinn.—A Seven Stories Press 1st ed.
p. cm.
ISBN 1-58322-049-6 (pbk.)
1. United States—History, Military—20th century. 2. United States—Foreign relations—20th century. 3. Zinn, Howard, 1922–   —Political and social views. 4. War—Moral and ethical aspects. 5. War and society—United States. I. Title.
E745.Z56 2000   00-032985
171'.42—dc21

9 8 7 6 5 4 3 2 1

College professors may order examination copies of Seven Stories Press titles for a free six-month trial period. To order, visit www.sevenstories.com/textbook, or fax on school letterhead to (212) 226-1411.

Printed in Canada

Contents

PART
1

On Remembering

1

The Massacres of History

I suppose that this essay is not just a reminder that there are massacres in American history which deserve to be remembered as much, or even more, than the famous Boston Massacre. It is also a commentary on how history itself is "massacred" by the omission of important, often embarrassing episodes—that is, embarrassing to those who insist that the nation's record must be kept clean, that the myth of American exceptionalism must be retained, that we are different and better than other nations.

This spring I was invited to participate in a symposium in Boston at historic Faneuil Hall (named after a slave trader but the site of many abolitionist meetings). The topic was to be the Boston Massacre. I hesitated a moment, then said, yes, I would speak, but only if I could also speak about other massacres in American history.

It was clear to me that the Boston Massacre, which took place on March 5, 1770, when British troops killed five colonists, is a much-remembered, indeed over-remembered event. Even the word "massacre" is a bit of an exaggeration; Webster's Collegiate Dictionary says the word denotes "wholesale slaughter."

Still, there is no denying the ugliness of a militia firing into a crowd, using as its rationale the traditional claim of trigger-happy police—that the crowd was "unruly" (as it undoubtedly was). John Adams, who was defense lawyer for the British soldiers and secured their acquittal, described the crowd as "a motley rabble of saucy boys, Negroes and mulattos, Irish teagues and outlandish jack tarrs."

Adams could hardly have expressed more clearly that the race and class of the victims (one of the dead, Crispus Attucks, was a mulatto) made their lives less precious. This was only one of many instances in which the Founding Fathers registered their desire to keep revolutionary fervor under the control of the more prosperous classes.

Ten thousand Bostonians (out of a total population of 16,000) marched in the funeral procession for the victims of the Massacre. And the British, hoping not to provoke more anger, pulled their troops out of Boston. Undoubtedly, the incident helped build sentiment for independence.

Still, I wanted to discuss other massacres because it seemed to me that concentrating attention on the Boston Massacre would be a painless exercise in patriotic fervor. There is no surer way to obscure the deep divisions of race and class in American history than by uniting us in support of the American Revolution and all its symbols (like Paul Revere's stark etching of the soldiers shooting into the crowd).

I suggested to the people assembled at Faneuil Hall (the walls around us crowded with portraits of the Founding Fathers and the nation's military heroes) that there were other massacres, forgotten or dimly remembered, that deserved to be recalled. These ignored episodes could tell us much about racial hysteria and class struggle, about shameful moments in our continental and overseas expansion, so that we can see ourselves more clearly, more honestly.

Why, for instance, was there not a symposium on what we might call the "Taino Massacre," perpetrated by Columbus and his fellow conquistadors, which annihilated the native population of Hispaniola. (Of several million living on that island—now Haiti and the Dominican Republic—by 1550, perhaps 50,000 were left)?

Or the "Pequot Massacre" of 1636, when our Puritan ancestors (well, I am stretching my ancestry a little), in an expedition led by Captain John Mason, set fire to a village of Pequot Indians on the Connecticut shore of Long Island Sound?

"Those that scaped the fire were slaine with the sword, some hewed to pieces... and very few escaped," wrote a contemporary, William Bradford, in his *History of the Plymouth Plantation.* And the Puritan theologian Cotton Mather wrote: "It was supposed that no less than 600 Pequot souls were brought down to hell that day." Mather was an expert on the destination of souls.

The massacres of Indians by the armies of the United States—in Colorado in 1864, in Montana in 1870, in South Dakota in 1890, to cite just a few—were massacres in the most literal sense, that is, wholesale slaughter in each case of hundreds of unarmed men, women, and children. The number of those events cannot be counted, and should by that fact be a subject for intense scrutiny.

The results of such an investigation would be as sobering to young Americans as the story of the Boston Massacre is inspiring. And sobriety about our national sins (sorry to use Dr. Mather's terminology) might be very instructive at a time when we need to consider what role we will play in the world this next century.

What of the massacres of African Americans, whether by official acts or by white mobs, with the collaboration of government officials? I will just cite two of many.

In the first months of the nation's entrance into World War II, an article called "The Massacre of East St. Louis" appeared in the NAACP publication, *Crisis,* written by W.E.B. DuBois and Martha Gruening. In that poor Illinois city, African Americans had been hired to replace whites, and hysteria took hold. (Job desperation was a common cause of mob violence, as when whites attacked Chinese miners in Rock Spring,

Wyoming, in 1885, killing twenty-five). The black section of East St. Louis became the object of attack by a white mob, leaving 6,000 homeless, perhaps 200 blacks dead, and mangled bodies found floating in the Mississippi River. Josephine Baker, the St. Louis–born entertainer who decided she could not live in this country, said at the time: "The very idea of America makes me shake and tremble and gives me nightmares." In July, thousands of African Americans marched silently, down Fifth Avenue to the roll of drums, with signs addressed to President Wilson: "MR. PRESIDENT, WHY NOT MAKE AMERICA SAFE FOR DEMOCRACY?"

In 1921, in Tulsa, Oklahoma, planes dropped nitroglycerin on a thirty-six-block black business district, destroying hundreds of businesses, more than 1,000 homes, twenty churches, a hospital, libraries, schools. The number of black people killed was estimated by some in the hundreds, by others in the thousands. Bodies were put into mass graves, stuffed into mine shafts, or thrown into the river.

Nor do our history books take much notice of workers killed by police and militia. I thought I knew about many of these events, but I keep learning about more. I did not know until recently about the Bay View Massacre in Milwaukee, which took place May 5, 1886 (the day after the Haymarket bombing in Chicago). On that day, striking steel workers, marching toward a mill in the Bay View section of Milwaukee, were intercepted by a squad of militia, who fired point blank into the strikers, killing seven.

A year later, in the fall of 1897, there was a coal strike in Pennsylvania. Immigrant Austrians, Hungarians, Italians, and Germans were brought in to break it. But the strikebreakers themselves soon organized and went on strike. Marching toward the Lattimer mine, they refused to disperse. The sheriff and his deputies opened fire and killed nineteen of them. Most were shot in the back.

When, the following year, the press set out to create a national excitement over the mysterious sinking of the battleship Maine in Havana harbor, a machinists' journal pointed to the Lattimer Massacre, saying that the deaths of workers resulted in no such uproar. It pointed out that "the carnival of carnage that takes place every day, month and year in the realm of industry, the thousands of useful lives that are annually sacrificed to the Moloch of greed...brings forth no shout for vengeance and reparation."

Better known, but still absent from the mainstream history books, is the Ludlow Massacre of 1914. Two companies of National Guardsmen, their pay underwritten by the Rockefeller interests that owned the Colorado Fuel & Iron Corporation, launched a military attack on the miners' tent colony, where 1,000 men, women, and children lived. The Guardsmen poured machine-gun fire into the tents, then burned them. Eleven children and two women died in the conflagration.

One of the many strikes of the Depression years was against Republic Steel in Chicago in 1937. Police began firing at a picket line and continued firing as the workers fled, killing ten in what came to be known as the Memorial Day Massacre.

Even less likely to enter the history books are the atrocities the United States commits overseas. High school and college texts usually deal at length with the three-month Spanish American War, portraying the United States as liberating Cuba from Spain and admiring Theodore Roosevelt's exploits with the "Rough Riders." But they rarely pay important attention to the eight-year war to conquer the Philippines, a bloody affair that in many ways resembled the war in Vietnam. (The United States killed hundreds of thousands of Filipinos in the war, but U.S. casualties were under 5,000.)

In 1906, an American military detachment attacked a village of Filipino Moslems ("Moros") living in the hollow of a mountain in one of the southern islands. Every one of 600 men, women, and children were killed. This was the Moro Massacre, which drew an angry response from Mark Twain and other anti-imperialist Americans.

In his capacity as vice-president of the Anti-Imperialist League, Twain wrote: "We have pacified thousands of the islanders and buried them, destroyed their fields, burned their villages, turned their widows and orphans out-of-doors, furnished heartbreak by exile to dozens of disagreeable patriots, and subjugated the remaining ten million by Benevolent Assimilation."

Those of us who were of age during the Vietnam War remember the My Lai Massacre of 1968, in which a company of American soldiers poured automatic rifle fire into groups of unarmed villagers, killing perhaps 500 people, many of them women and children. But when I spoke last fall to a group of 100 high school honors students in history and asked who knew about the My Lai Massacre, no one raised a hand.

My Lai was not a unique event. An Army colonel charged with covering up the My Lai incident told reporters: "Every unit of brigade size has its My Lai hidden someplace."

And if the word "massacre" means indiscriminate mass slaughter of innocent people, is it not reasonable to call the bombings of Hiroshima and Nagasaki "massacres," as well as the fire-bombing of Tokyo and the destruction of Dresden and other German cities?

In Ignazio Silone's novel *Fontemara,* about peasants under Italian fascism, the resistance movement distributed leaflets just giving out information that had been suppressed, and then simply asking: "Che fare?" What shall we do? ("They have killed Berardo Viola. What shall we do? They have taken away our water? What shall we do? They violate our women in the name of the law. What shall we do?") When our government, our media, and our schools select certain events for remembering and ignore others, we have the responsibility to supply the missing information. Just to tell untold truths has a powerful effect, because people with ordinary common sense may then be led to ask themselves and others: "What shall we do?"

2

Veterans Day

As I watched Veterans Day, November 11, once again being turned into a day, not just to honor veterans, but to honor war, I was moved to write this op-ed piece, which appeared in the Greenwich, Connecticut *Times*, the Long Beach, California *Press Telegram*, *The Miami Herald*, *The Arizona Daily Star*, and other newspapers.

Let's go back to the beginning of Veterans Day. It used to be Armistice Day, because at the eleventh hour of the eleventh day of the eleventh month of 1918, the first World War came to an end.

We must not forget that conflict. It revealed the essence of war, of all wars, because however "just" or "humanitarian" may be the claims, at the irreducible core of all war is the slaughter of the innocent, organized by national leaders, accompanied by lies. World War I was its epitome, as generals and politicians sent young men forward from their trenches, bayonets fixed, to gain a few miles, even a few yards, at frightful cost.

In July of 1916 the British General Douglas Haig ordered eleven divisions of English soldiers to climb out of their trenches and move toward the German lines. The six German divisions opened up with their machine guns. Of the 110,000 who attacked, more than half were killed or wounded—all those bodies strewn on no man's land, the ghostly territory between the contending trenches. That scenario went on for years. In the first battle of the Marne there were a million casualties, 500,000 on each side.

The soldiers began to rebel, which is always the most heroic thing soldiers can do, for which they should be given medals. In the French army, out of 112 divisions, 68 would have mutinies. Fifty men would be shot by firing squads.

Three of those executions became the basis for Stanley Kubrick's antiwar masterpiece, *Paths of Glory*. In that film, a pompous general castigates his soldiers for retreating, and talks of "patriotism." Kirk Douglas, the lieutenant-colonel who defends his men, enrages the general by quoting the famous lines of Samuel Johnson: "Patriotism is the last refuge of a scoundrel."

The supposed moral justification of that war (the evil Kaiser, the Belgian babies) disintegrated quickly after it ended, with sudden recognition of the ten million dead in the mud of France, and the gassed, shellshocked and limbless veterans confronting the world. ("Where are your legs that used to run, when you went for to carry a gun. Oh I fear your dancin' days are done...Johnny I hardly knew ya...")

The ugliness of that war was uncomplicated by the moral righteousness that made later wars, from World War II on, unsullied in our memory, or at least acceptable. Vietnam was the stark exception. But even there our national leaders have worked hard to smother what they called "the Vietnam syndome," to forget what we learned at that war's end: that our leaders cannot be trusted, that modern war is inevitably a war against civilians and particularly children, that only a determined citizenry can stop the government when it embarks on mass murder.

Our decent impulse, to recognize the ordeal of our veterans, has been used to obscure the fact that they died, they were crippled, for no good cause other than the power and profit of a few. Veterans Day, instead of an occasion for denouncing war, has become an occasion for bringing out the flags, the uniforms, the martial music, the patriotic speeches reeking with hypocrisy. Those who name holidays, playing on our genuine feeling for veterans, have turned a day that celebrated the end of a horror, into a day to honor militarism.

As a combat veteran myself, of a "good war," against fascism, I do not want the recognition of my service to be used as a glorification of war. At the end of that war, in which fifty million died, the people of the world should have shouted "Enough!" We should have decided that from that moment on, we would renounce war—and there would be no Korean War, Vietnam War, Panama War, Grenada War, Gulf War, Balkan War.

The reason for such a decision is that war in our time—whatever "humanitarian" motives are claimed by our political leaders—is always a war against children: the child amputees created by our bombing of Yugoslavia, the hundreds of thousands of Iraqi children dead as a result of our post-war sanctions. Veterans Day should be an occasion for a national vow: no more war victims on the other side; no more war veterans on our side.

PART 2

On Kosovo
and Yugoslavia

3

Their Atrocities
and Ours

We have become accustomed to the misuse of language by
political and military leaders to deceive the public. I suppose it
is a tribute to the humanity of ordinary people that horrible
acts must be camouflaged in a thicket of deceptive words in
order to justify them. This op-ed piece appeared in the *Boston
Globe* and several other newspapers around the country at the
time of the bombing of Yugoslavia. Technically, it was NATO—
the North Atlantic Treaty Organization—that was carrying on
the bombing, but in reality (another obfuscation) it was the
United States.

There was a headline this morning in my home town newspaper, the
Boston Globe: "PENTAGON DEFENDS AIRSTRIKE ON VIL-
LAGE. U.S. SAYS KOSOVARS WERE 'HUMAN SHIELDS'."

That brought back the ugliest of memories: of My Lai and other
Vietnam massacres, justified by "the Vietnamese babies are concealing
hand grenades." And Madeleine Albright's response after Pakistani troops
had fired into a crowd of Somali citizens: "They are using civilians as
shields."

Milosovic has committed atrocities. Therefore it is okay for us to commit atrocities. He is terrorizing the Albanians in Kosovo. Therefore we can terrorize the population of cities and villages in Yugoslavia.

I get e-mail messages from Yugoslav opponents of Milosovic, who demonstrated against him in the streets of Belgrade (before the air strikes began), who tell me their children cannot sleep at night, terrified by the incessant bombing. They tell of the loss of light, of water, of the destruction of the basic sources of life for ordinary people.

To the bloodthirsty Thomas Friedman of *The New York Times*, all Serbs must be punished, without mercy, because they have "tacitly sanctioned" the deeds of their leaders. That is a novel definition of war guilt. Can we now expect an Iraqi journalist to call for bombs placed in every American supermarket on the ground that all of us have "tacitly sanctioned" the hundreds of thousands of deaths in Iraq caused by our eight-year long embargo.

Official terrorism, whether used abroad or at home, by jet bombers or by the police, is always given an opportunity by the press to explain itself, as is never done for ordinary terrorists. The thirty one prisoners and nine guards massacred at Governor Rockefeller's orders in the Attica uprising; the twenty-eight women and children of the organization MOVE, killed in a fire after their homes were bombed by Philadelphia police; the eighty-six men, women, and children of the Waco compound who died in an attack ordered by the Clinton Administration; the African immigrant murdered by a gang of policemen in New York—all of these events had explanations which, however absurd, are dutifully given time and space by the media.

One of these explanations is in terms of numbers, and we have heard both Clinton and his forked-tongue counterpart Jamie Shea pass off the bombing of Yugoslav civilians by telling us the Serb police have killed more Albanians than we have killed Serbs (although as the air strikes multiply, the numbers are getting closer). They have killed more than we have, so it's okay to bomb not just Serbs but Albanian refugees, not just adults but children, and to use the cluster bombs which have caused unprecedented amputations in Kosovo hospitals.

There were those who defended the 1945 firestorm bombing of Dresden (100,000 dead?—we can't be sure) by pointing to the Holocaust. As if one atrocity deserves another. And with no chance at all that one could prevent the other (just as our bombings have done nothing to stop the mayhem in Kosovo, indeed have intensified it). I have heard the deaths of several hundred thousand Japanese citizens in the atomic strikes on Hiroshima and Nagasaki justified by the terrible acts of the Japanese military in that war.

I suppose if we consider the millions of casualties of all the wars started by national leaders these past fifty years as "tacitly" supported by their populations, some righteous God who made the mistake of reading Friedman might well annihilate the human race.

The television networks, filling our screen with heartrending photos of the Albanian refugees—and those stories must not be ignored—have not given us a full picture of the human suffering we have caused by our bombing.

An e-mail came to me, a message from Professor Djordje Vidanovic, a professor of linguistics and semantics at the University of Nis: "The little town of Aleksinac, 20 miles away from my home town, was hit last night will full force. The local hospital was hit and a whole street was simply wiped off. What I know for certain is 6 dead civilians and more than 50 badly hurt. There was no military target around whatsoever."

That was an "accident." As was the bombing of the Chinese Embassy. As was the bombing of a civilian train on a bridge over the Juzna Morava River, as was the bombing of Albanian refugees on a road in southern Kosovo, as was the destruction of a civilian bus with twenty four dead including four children (there was a rare press description of the gruesome scene by Paul Watson of the *Los Angeles Times*).

Some stories come through despite the inordinate attention to NATO propaganda, omnipresent on CNN and other networks (and the shameless Jamie Shea announced we bombed a television station in Belgrade because it gave out propaganda). *The New York Times* reported the demolition of four houses in the town of Merdare by anti-personnel bombs "killing five people, including Bozina Tosovic, 30, and his 11-month old daughter, Bojana. His wife, 6 months pregnant, is in the hospital.

Steven Erlanger reported, also in *The New York Times*, that NATO missiles killed at least eleven people in a residential area of Surdulica, a town in southern Serbia. He described "the mounded rubble across narrow Zmaj Jovina Street, where Aleksandar Milic, 37, died on Tuesday. Mr. Milic's wife, Vesna, 35, also died. So did his mother and his two children, Miljana, 15 and Vladimir, 11—all of them killed about noon when an errant NATO bomb obliterated their new house and the cellar in which they were sheltering."

Are these "accidents," as NATO and U.S. officials solemnly assure us?

One day in 1945, I dropped canisters of napalm on a village in France. I have no idea how many villagers died, but I did not mean to kill them. Can I absolve what I did as "an accident"? Aerial bombings have as inevitable consequences the killing of civilians, and this is foreseeable, even if the details about who will be the victims cannot be predicted.

The word "accident" is used to exonerate vicious actions. If I race my car at eighty miles an hour through a street crowded with children, and kill ten of them, can I call that an "accident"? The deaths and mutilations caused by the bombing campaign in Yugoslavia are not accidents, but the inevitable result of a deliberate and cruel campaign against the people of that country.

When I read a few weeks ago that cluster bombs are being used against Yugoslavia, I felt a special horror. These have hundreds of shrapnel-like metal fragments which enter the body and cannot easily be removed, causing unbearable pain. Serb children have picked up unexploded bombs and been mutilated as they exploded. I remember being in Hanoi in 1968 and visiting hospitals where children lay in agony, victims of a similar weapon—cluster bombs—their bodies full of tiny pellets.

Two sets of atrocities—two campaigns of terrorism—ours and theirs. Both must be condemned. But for that, both must be acknowledged, and if one is given enormous attention, and the other passed over with official explanations given respectful attention, it becomes impossible to make a balanced moral judgement.

There was an extraordinary report by Tim Weiner in *The New York Times* contrasting the scene in Belgrade with that in Washington, where the NATO summit was taking place. "In Belgrade...Gordana Ristic, 33, was preparing to spend another night in the basement-cum-bomb shelter of her apartment building. 'It was a really horrible night last night. There were explosions every few minutes after 2 AM.... I'm sorry that your leaders are not willing to read history.'

"A reporter read to her from Clinton's speeches at the summit meeting. She sounded torn between anger and tears. 'This is the bottom to which civilization, in which I believed, has gone. Clinton is playing a role, singing a song in an opera. It kills me.' As she slept, NATO's leaders dined on soft-shell crabs and spring lamb in the East Room of the White House. Dessert was a little chocolate globe. Jessye Norman sang arias. And as the last limousine left, near midnight. Saturday morning's all-clear sounded in Belgrade."

Yes, Milosovic should stand in the dock to answer for war crimes. Clinton, Albright, Cohen, and Clark should stand with him.

There is another factor which we as Americans must consider when we confront the atrocities on both sides. We bear a moral responsibility in any situation to the extent that we have the capacity to affect that situation. In the case of the Milosovic cruelties against the Kosovars, our capacity to intervene (which may have been greater at an earlier stage, before we rushed to bomb) is very limited, unless we go into a full scale ground war, in which the resulting mayhem will far exceed the tragedy that has already taken place. But as Americans we have a direct responsibility for the cruelties our government is inflicting on innocent people in Yugoslavia.

We are seeing liberals and even some radicals, forgetting their own harsh criticism of the controlled press, succumb to the barrage of information about the horrors inflicted on the people of Kosovo. That information is isolated from its context—the human consequences of our bombing campaign, the record of the United States government in ignoring or abetting "ethnic cleansing" in various parts of the world, the refusal of the U.S. and NATO to respond to reasonable and negotiable proposals from the other side. And so those who should know better are led to support violent solutions.

George Seldes, that fierce exposer of the press, and Upton Sinclair, who wrote of the prostitution of the newspapers in *The Brass Check*, both lost their sense of proportion as they were inundated with Allied propaganda in World War I, and found themselves supporting a stupid military debacle which ended with ten million dead. Seldes later wrote (I owe this to the indefatigable Seldes' fan Ken McCarthy): "Of the first war years I will say just this: I made a total fool of myself when I accepted as true the news reports from New York and Europe which by their volume and repetition overwhelmed what little objective intelligence I had..."If the Serbian military are killing and expelling the Albanians in Kosovo, it is a reasonable reaction to say: "We must do something." But if that is the only information we are getting, a quick jump is made to: "We must bomb" or "We must invade." If we don't want to perpetuate the violence on both sides, we will have to demand of our leaders that they discard their macho arrogance("We will win!" "Milosovic will lose!" "We are the superpower!" "Our credibility is at stake!"), that they stop bombing and start talking.

There will at some point be a negotiated end to the violence in Yugoslavia. But how many people on both sides will die needlessly and horribly in the interim? That depends on how quickly the American people can raise a powerful cry of protest against the actions of our government.

4

A Diplomatic Solution

Many people on the American Left, who had been united in their opposition to the Vietnam War and the Gulf War, were divided on what to do when the Milosevic regime in Yugoslavia attacked people in Kosovo for wanting independence, committing atrocities, driving people from their homes. The Clinton Administration responded with a bombing campaign, and I tried in this essay to sort out the moral issues.

A friend wrote to ask my opinion on Kosovo. He said many people were turning to him for answers, and he didn't know what to say, so he was turning to me (knowing, I guess, that I always have something to say, right or wrong).

Several things seem clear to me, and they don't fit easily together in a way that points to a clean solution:

Milosevic and his Serb forces are committing atrocities.

But bombing won't help. It can only make things worse, and that is already evident. It is creating more victims, on both sides.

The Kosovo Liberation Army may not represent the wishes of the Kosovar people. It turned to armed struggle to gain independence, ruthlessly putting its countrymen at risk, when a protracted nonviolent campaign of resistance was already going on and should have continued.

I think of South Africa, where a decision to engage in out-and-out armed struggle would have led to a bloody civil war with huge casualties, most of them black. Instead, the African National Congress decided to put up with apartheid longer, but wage a long-term campaign of attrition, with strikes, sabotage, economic sanctions, and international pressure. It worked.

The United States does not have a humanitarian aim in this situation. U.S. foreign policy has never been guided by such concerns, but by political power, economic interest, and sometimes a motive more elusive—machismo. (We want to show the world we are Number One, as President after President has reiterated since the beginning of the Vietnam War.)

The hypocrisy of the Clinton Administration is evident after just a glance at recent history. When Chechnya rebelled, demanding independence from Russia just as Kosovo wants it from Yugoslavia now, the Russian army moved in and did terrible things to the people of Chechnya. Clinton did not oppose this. In fact, in fielding one reporter's question, he compared the situation to the American Civil War, when Lincoln would not permit the Confederacy to secede.

There is no sensible military solution to the ethnic cleansing. It could be stopped only by putting in a large ground force, which would mean a full-scale war, which would greatly multiply the present violence.

What is happening to the people of Kosovo is heartrending, and I think the only solution is a diplomatic one, forgetting the treaty the United States tried to force on Serbia. It will take a new agreement, in which the Kosovars will have to settle for some form of autonomy, but no guarantee of independence: a compromise in order to have peace. And the most likely way this diplomatic solution can come about is through the intercession of Russia, which should exercise its influence over the Serbs.

The United States is violating the U.N. Charter. But any reference to international law may appear futile, since the United States has rendered it worthless for fifty years. The bombing also violates the U.S. Constitution, which requires a declaration of war, and we are certainly waging war.

The United States and NATO (which is the creation of the United States and does its bidding) are floundering, and in the process they are doing enormous damage to human beings. This situation will require the citizens of the NATO countries—especially in the United States—to shout their protest at what is going on, and to demand a diplomatic solution. When a nation issues ultimatums, it leaves no room for compromise and ensures that war will continue.

We learned from Vietnam that the ruthlessness of leaders, the stupidity of "experts," must be countered by the courage, good sense, and persistence of the citizenry.

PART 3

On Iraq

5

One Iraqi's Story

My reaction to the December 1998 bombing of Iraq by the Clinton Administration was sent out over the Internet, although I was not aware of this until I received an e-mail from an Iraqi physician living in London. It cut through the abstraction of "bombing" to see what happened to a single family. After my article appeared, a number of Americans began a correspondence with Dr. Al-Obaidi.

As Bill Clinton and Tony Blair were bombing Iraq on December 20, I received an e-mail message from England:

Dear Professor Zinn,

I am an Iraqi citizen who sought refuge here in the U.K. because of the brutality of Saddam's regime, which, within two years, killed my innocent old father and my youngest brother, who left a wife and three children....

I am writing to you to let you know that during the second day of bombarding Iraq, a cruise missile hit my parents' house in a suburb of Baghdad. My mother, my sister-in-law (wife of my deceased brother), and her three children were all killed instantly.

Such a tragedy shocked me to such an extent I lost my tears. I am crying without tears. I wish I could show my eyes and express my severe and painful suffering to every American and British [citizen]. I wish I could tell my story to those sitting in the American Administration, the U.N., and at Number 10 Downing Street. For the sake of Monica and Clinton, my family has to pay this expensive and invaluable cost. I am wondering, who will compensate me for my loss? I wish I could go to Iraq to drop some tears on my mother's grave, who always wanted to see me before her death....

Please convey my story to all those whom you think can still see the truth in their eyes and can hear this tragic story with their ears.

Sincerely yours,

Dr. Mohammed Al-Obaidi

It seems to me this conveys with terrible clarity that Saddam Hussein and the leaders of our government have much in common: They are both visiting death and suffering on the people of Iraq.

In response to the possibility that Saddam Hussein may have "weapons of mass destruction" and the additional possibility that he may use them in the future, the United States, in the present, shows no compunction about using weapons of mass destruction: cruise missiles, B-52 bombers, and, most of all, economic sanctions, which have resulted in the deaths of hundreds of thousands of Iraqi children.

With the December bombings, Bill Clinton was perfectly willing to kill a number (how many we do not know) of Iraqis, including five members of Dr. Mohammed Al-Obaidi's family. Why? "To send a message," his Administration said.

Would the United States be willing to take the lives of a similar number of Americans "to send a message"? Are Iraqis less worthy of life than we are? Are their children less innocent than ours?

President Clinton said that Saddam Hussein poses a "clear and present danger" to the peace of the world. Whatever danger Saddam Hussein may pose in the future, he is not a clear and present danger to the peace of the world. We are. Notice the President's use of this much-abused term. The Supreme Court of the United States invoked it to justify the imprisonment of people distributing leaflets protesting the U.S. entrance into World War I. Cold Warriors used it to justify McCarthyism and the nuclear arms race. Now President Clinton has pulled it off the shelf for equally disreputable purposes.

President Clinton also said that other nations besides Iraq have weapons of mass destruction, but Iraq alone has used them. He could say this only to a population deprived of history. No nation in the world possesses greater weapons of mass destruction than ours, and none has used them more often, or with greater loss of civilian life. In Hiroshima and Nagasaki, more than 100,000 civilians died after the United States dropped atom bombs on them. In Korea and Vietnam, millions died after the United States dropped "conventional" weapons on them. So who are we to brag about our restraint in using weapons of mass destruction?

The U.S. penchant for bombing blots out the government's ability to focus on humanitarian crises—and not just in Iraq. When Hurricane Mitch devastated Central America, leaving tens of thousands dead and more than a million people homeless, there was a desperate need for helicopters to transport people to safety and deliver food and medicine. Mexico supplied sixteen helicopters to Honduras. The United States supplied twelve. At the same time, the Pentagon dispatched a huge armada—helicopters, transport planes, B-52s—to the Middle East.

Every cruise missile used to bomb Iraq cost about $1 million, and the Pentagon used about 250 of them: a quarter of a billion dollars in cruise missiles alone. At the same time, the Knight-Ridder News Service reported that the Department of Defense, on the eve of winter, had stopped distributing millions of blankets to homeless programs around the country. The Senate Armed Services Committee had not approved the appropriation. According to the news dispatch, "The Congressional committee said the cost of the blanket program diverted needed money from weaponry."

Thus, our weapons kill people abroad, while homeless people freeze at home. Are not our moral priorities absurdly distorted?

When I received the message from Dr. Al-Obaidi, I tried to meet his request by reading from his letter on a number of radio interviews in various parts of the country. I have written to him to tell him that. Nothing, of course, can restore his family. All we can do is try to convey to the American public the human consequences of our government's repeated use of violence for political and economic gain. When enough of them see and feel what is happening to people just like us—to families, to children—we may see the beginning of a new movement in this country against militarism and war.

6

Bombing Iraq

In February of 1998, as the United States was on the verge of sending bombers over Iraq, three of the government's leading propagandists—Secretary of State Madeleine Albright, Secretary of Defense William Cohen, and National Security Adviser Samuel Berger—spoke at a town hall meeting in Columbus, Ohio to explain why the United States had to bomb Iraq. But in the question period, which the organizers of the gathering had tried to control, got out of control when an opponent of the bombing took the floor to question Madeleine Albright. He asked why the United States had singled out Iraq for bombing when other nations—allies of the United States—possessed weapons of mass destruction and did not face punishment. Albright stammered, unable to coherently answer, and this was seen on television screens across the country. This incident apparently called a temporary halt to the plans for bombing, although ten months later, the bombers went into action, prompting this op-ed piece of mine, which appeared in several newspapers around the country.

All of us who have been taken aback by our government's hysterical rush to violence in the Middle East can now be taken forward by the courage of a lone voice in Congress speaking out against the madness. The voice was that of Rep. Cynthia McKinney of Georgia, who, on *Newshour with Jim Lehrer* last week, faced off, with facts, logic, and passion, three fellow legislators who stammered and stuttered vainly to defend aggressive action against Iraq.

The illogic and immorality of bombing Iraq can be stated very simply: we will, with certainty, be killing innocent people (many more than were killed by Timothy McVeigh in Oklahoma), with no certainty at all that we will be achieving the declared objective of destroying Saddam Hussein's capacity to unleash "weapons of mass destruction."

There is not even certainty about the existence of such weapons in Iraq, or, if they do exist, about their location. Retired marine general Bernard Trainor, raised questions recently in the *Boston Globe*:

> The first question is how accurate is our intelligence that Saddam possesses, and is manufacturing, weapons of mass destruction, particularly biological weapons? If true, does possession alone constitute a "clear and present danger" to the international community, as Secretary of State Madeline Albright claims?... We have not been shown specific evidence to back up the claim."

The United Nations Special Commission which is charged with the job of inspecting Iraq's weaponry, has said that Iraq does not have the missile capacity to deliver chemical or biological weapons. This was echoed recently by an Israeli military man. And General Charles A. Horner, who commanded air forces in the Gulf War, wrote in *The New York Times* recently:

> Ultimately, neither an air war nor a ground invasion would solve the conflict over weapons of mass destruction.... Biological spores can be grown in easily hidden laboratories. Chemical weapons can be constructed in the most primitive of sites.... Making matters worse, attacks on weapons sites could easily spew plumes of biological or chemical toxins into the air, increasing the damage."

To put it another way, if there is a "clear and present danger," it does not come from Saddam Hussein, but from our own government, which is on the verge of killing large numbers of Iraqi civilians, and unleashing violence whose consequences cannot be predicted.

Can the American public accept a gross act of immorality perpetrated in our name? Have we not been through this before? Did it not take us years to awaken to the fact that in Vietnam we were killing, maiming, napalming men, women, children because our leaders assured us this was being done to contain "the threat of Communism"—as if six-year-old children, and eighty-year-old women were our enemies? Should we not raise a cry now, before the bombs begin to fall?

There is gross hypocrisy in Washington, engaged in by Clinton, Cohen, Albright, and all those Republicans and Democrats in Congress who are going along like sheep. I am referring to the fact that there are many countries in the world that possess weapons of mass destruction, countries which are run by tyrannies equal to that of Saddam Hussein—Turkey, Saudi Arabia, Indonesia, Pakistan, China—but we do not speak of that because they are "friends"—either military allies or profitable markets.

Further hypocrisy: these weapons of mass destruction have been supplied to tyrannical governments all over the world by our own government. True, Saddam Hussein is a tyrant who oppresses his own people. But the U.S. has given huge quantities of arms to Indonesia, enabling it to commit genocide against the people of East Timor, on a scale of terror far beyond what Saddam Hussein has ever done.

To say that we are implementing United Nations policy is simply not true. The U.N. is authorized to carry out inspections; it has not authorized a unilateral bombing campaign. Such a campaign would indeed violate the U.N. Charter, which permits acts of aggression, like bombing, only in clear cases of self-defense. This is not such a case.

A bombing campaign would compound the horrors we have already committed in Iraq by our policy of sanctions; the United Nations itself has estimated that perhaps a million people in Iran, half of them children, have died as a result of the lack of food and medicine caused by these sanctions.

Whatever claim we have to democracy is being shattered by the rush to war (and a bombing campaign is unmistakably an act of war). Aside from the ignoring of the Constitutional requirement of a Congressional declaration of war—to which we have become accustomed in Korea, Vietnam, Grenada, Panama—we are allowing a small number of political leaders to push the American people into war without a real national debate, without a full airing of the issues. The reason for that is clear: if the American people had access to the facts, could listen to different points of view, and time for reasoned judgment, they would call a halt to our leaders' lust for violence.

PART 4

On Libya

7

Terrorism Over Tripoli

In April of 1986, a bomb exploded in a discotheque in West Berlin, killing two people, one an American soldier. It was unquestionably an act of terrorism. Libya's tyrannical leader, Muommar Khadafi, had a record of involvement in terrorism, although in this case there seemed to be no clear evidence of who was responsible. Nevertheless, President Reagan ordered that bombers be sent over Libya's capital of Tripoli, killing perhaps a hundred people, almost all civilians. I wrote this piece, which could not find publication in the press, to argue against the principle of retaliation. I am always furious at the killing of innocent people for some political cause, but I wanted to broaden the definition of terrorism to include governments, which are guilty of terrorism far more often, and on an infinitely larger scale, than bands of revolutionaries or nationalists. The essay became part of a collection of my writings entitled *Failure to Quit,* published in 1993 by Common Courage Press.

"Indeed, I tremble for my country when I reflect that God is just." Thomas Jefferson wrote that in *Notes from Virginia.*

Those words came to mind as I listened to the announcement from our government that it hd bombed the city of Tripoli.

We live in a world in which we are asked to make a moral choice between one kind of terrorism and another. The government, the press, the politicians, are trying to convince us that Ronald Reagan's terrorism is morally superior to Muommar Khadafi's terrorism.

Of course, we don't call our actions that, but if terrorism is the deliberate killing of innocent people to make a political point, then our bombing a crowded city in Libya fits the definition as well as the bombing—by whoever did it—of a crowded discotheque in Berlin.

Perhaps the word deliberate shows the difference: when you plant a bomb in a discotheque, the death of bystanders is deliberate; when you drop bombs on a city, it is accidental. We can ease our conscience that way, but only by lying to ourselves. Because, when you bomb a city from the air, you know, absolutely know, that innocent people will die.

That's why Defense Secretary Weinberger, reaching for morality (his reach will never be long enough, given where he stands) talked of the air raid being organized in such a way as to "minimize" civilian casualties. That meant there would inevitably be civilian casualties, and Weinberger, Shultz, and Reagan were willing to have that happen, to make their point, as the discotheque terrorists were willing to have that happen, to make theirs.

In this case, the word "minimize" meant only about a hundred dead (the estimate of foreign diplomats in Tripoli), including infants and children, an eighteen-year-old college girl home for a visit, an unknown number of elderly people. None of these were terrorists, just as none of the people in the discotheque were responsible for whatever grievances are felt by Libyans or Palestinians.

Even if we assume that Khadafi was behind the discotheque bombing (and there is no evidence for this), and Reagan behind the Tripoli bombing (the evidence for this is absolute), then both are terrorists, but Reagan is capable of killing far more people than Khadafi. And he has.

Reagan, and Weinberger, and Secretary of State Shultz, and their admirers in the press and in Congress are congratulating themselves that the world's most heavily-armed nation can bomb with impunity (only two U.S. fliers dead, a small price to pay for psychic satisfaction) a fourth-rate nation like Libya.

Modern technology has outdistanced the Bible. "An eye for an eye" has become a hundred eyes for an eye, a hundred babies for a baby. The tough-guy columnists and anonymous editorial writers (there were a few courageous exceptions) who defended this, tried to wrap their moral nakedness in the American flag. But it dishonors the flag to wave it proudly over the killing of a college student, or a child sleeping in a crib.

There is no flag large enough to cover the shame of killing innocent people for a purpose which is unattainable. If the purpose is to stop terrorism, even the supporters of the bombing say it won't work; if the purpose is to gain respect for the United States, the result is the opposite: all over the world there is anger and indignation at Reagan's mindless, pointless, soulless violence. We have had Presidents just as violent. We have rarely had one so full of hypocritical pieties about "the right to life."

In this endless exchange of terrorist acts, each side claims it is "retaliating." We bombed Tripoli to retaliate for the discotheque. The discotheque may have been bombed to retaliate for our killing 35 Libyan seamen who were on a patrol boat in the Gulf of Sidra—in international waters, just as we were.

We were in the Gulf of Sidra supposedly to show Libya it must not engage in terrorism. And Libya says—indeed it is telling the truth in this instance—that the United States is an old hand at terrorism, having subsidized terrorist governments in Chile, Guatemala, and El Salvador, and right now subsidizing the terrorism of the contras against farmers, their wives and children, in Nicaragua.

Does a Western democracy have a better right to kill innocent people than a Middle Eastern dictatorship? Even if we were a perfect democracy that would not give us such a license. But the most cherished element of our democracy—the pluralism of dissenting voices, the marketplace of contending ideas—seems to disappear at a time like this, when the bombs fall, the flag waves, and everyone scurries, as Ted Kennedy did, to fall meek-ly behind "our commander-in-chief." We waited for moral leadership. But Gary Hart, John Kerry, Michael Dukakis, and Tip O'Neill all muttered their support. No wonder the Democratic Party is in such pathetic shape.

Where in national politics are the emulators of those two courageous voices at the time of the Gulf of Tonkin incident in Vietnam—Wayne Morse and Ernest Gruening—who alone in the Senate refused to go along with "our commander-in-chief" in that first big military strike that launched the ten-year shame of Vietnam?

And where was our vaunted "free press"? After the bombing, a beam-ing Shultz held a press conference for a group of obsequious reporters in Washington who buttered him up, who licked at his flanks, who didn't ask a single question about the morality of our action, about the civilians killed by our bombs in Tripoli. Where are the likes of I.F Stone, who did in his little newsletter for so many years what no big American daily would do—raise hard questions? Why did Anthony Lewis and Tom Wicker, who sometimes raise such questions—melt away?

Terrorism now has two names, world-wide. One is Khadafi. One is Reagan. In fact, that is a gross simplification. If Khadafi were gone, if Reagan were gone, terrorism would continue—it is a very old weapon of fanatics, whether they operate from secret underground headquarters, or from ornate offices in the capitols of the superpowers.

Too bad Khadafi's infant daughter died, one columnist wrote. Too bad, he said, but that's the game of war. Well, if that's the game, then let's get the hell out of it, because it is poisoning us morally, and not solving any problem. It is only continuing and escalating the endless cycle of retaliation which will one day, if we don't kick our habits, kill us all.

Let us hope that, even if this generation, its politicians, its reporters, its flag-wavers and fanatics, cannot change its ways, the children of the next generation will know better, having observed our stupidity. Perhaps they will understand that the violence running wild in the world cannot be stopped by more violence, that someone must say: we refuse to retal-iate, the cycle of terrorism stops here.

PART 5

On Vietnam

8

Remembering a War

This op-ed piece was suggested to me by the Progressive Media Project which serves the valuable purpose of sending out politically unorthodox op-ed pieces to newspapers all over the country. It appeared in half a dozen newspapers around the country, including the *Atlanta Constitution.* I thought it important to remind people of that immoral war, since there have been strenuous efforts by those in high places to make war palatable once again to the American public. President Bush, as he sent troops into the Middle East, proclaimed that the "Vietnam syndrome" (by which he meant the revulsion against war caused by the Vietnam experience, had been "buried in the sands of the Arabian peninsula." Let us hope not.

It was thirty years ago (January 30, 1968) that Daniel Berrigan, a Jesuit priest and poet teaching at Cornell, and I, once an Air Force bombardier and now a historian teaching at Boston University, traveled (illegally) to Hanoi. Our mission was to pick up the first three captured American pilots to be released by the North Vietnam government and bring them home.

It was the time of the Tet offensive, and we spent a week in Laos waiting for the battered World War II plane that flew six times a month from Saigon to Pnompenh to Vientiane to Hanoi to be able to leave the besieged airport in Saigon. Then, a week of intensive observation in North Vietnam, after which we flew back with the three airmen to Vientiane. They returned to the Air Force. We returned to the anti-war movement, Father Berrigan to a series of acts of civil disobedient protest that landed him in prison, I to a crowded schedule of teach-ins and demonstrations against the war.

Thirty years later, this might be a good time to reflect on what we might learn from that longest of our wars, the one which has brought agreement from both opponents of the war and political leaders who promulgated the war (Robert MacNamara being the most vivid recent example) that it was a shameful episode in our nation's history.

I do not pretend to be a cool and distant commentator, although I have read widely and listened carefully to all the major arguments. To me, the war was a disaster not, as some have said (MacNamara among them), because it could not be won. The dispatch of a huge army to a small country, the merciless bombing of both enemy and "friendly" territory, the deaths of perhaps three million people and destruction of a beautiful land, the brutal massacres at My Lai and other places, were morally indefensible, win or lose.

None of the "reasons" given to explain what we did—stopping the spread of Communism, defending an ally, fulfilling our "treaty obligations"—could stand up under examination. And even if any element of that explanation might be true—perhaps we could have a non-Communist corrupt government in South Vietnam instead of a Communist dictatorship there—would it justify the mass slaughter of Asian peasants and the deaths of 58,000 Americans, to say nothing of all those left blind, maimed, paralyzed on both sides?

Most Americans came to understand this. Their basic sense of decency came to the fore when they learned what was going on. As Kurt Vonnegut has said, responding to the old claim that violence is basic to "human nature," there is such a thing as original virtue, as well as original sin. The surveys of public opinion showed a steady growth of opposition to the war, in all sectors of the nation, In August of 1965, 61 percent of the population approved of the American involvement in Vietnam. By May of 1971 it was exactly reversed, now 61 percent thought our involvement was wrong.

Perhaps the most dramatic evidence of the change was that veterans coming back from Vietnam organized to oppose the war (Ron Kovic, for one, paralyzed, writing *Born on the Fourth of July*).

What have we learned that might be of use in our world today? I suggest the following as starters:

That with the indiscriminate nature of modern military technology (no such thing as a "smart bomb," it turns out) all wars are wars against civilians, and are therefore inherently immoral. This is true even when a war is considered "just," because it is fought against a tyrant, against an aggressor, to correct a stolen boundary. (The "good war" against Saddam Hussein has succeeded only in bringing about the deaths of hundreds of thousands of Iraqi children, according to United Nations reports.)

That political leaders all over the world should not be trusted when they urge their people to war claiming superior knowledge and expertise. The North Vietnamese leaders sacrificed their people for "socialism," whose principles they then betrayed. The recently released tapes of Kennedy, Johnson, and Nixon, all show a terrifying common thread: that they were willing to watch soldiers and civilians die in large numbers while they calculated the effect on their re-election of stopping those deaths by withdrawing from Vietnam.

9

The CIA, Rockefeller, and the Boys in the Club

The CIA, it is generally understood by now (1996), has a long and dirty record of violating, again and again, norms of moral behavior: overthrowing governments, installing military dictatorships, planning the assassinations of foreign leaders, spying on American citizens, interfering in foreign elections, causing the deaths of large numbers of innocent people. In 1975, at the end of the Vietnam War, some of its activities were just coming to the fore, and to quiet further inquiry an investigating commission was set up under Nelson Rockefeller. When the commission released its report, I wrote a column (June 7, 1975) for the *Boston Globe*.

"Rockefeller Inquiry Clears CIA of Major Violations" was the headline in *The New York Times*. Now we can relax. Except for one troubling question: who will clear Rockefeller?

All these fellows go around clearing one another. It seems that only at the top levels of government is serious attention paid to the principle that criminals should be tried by juries of their peers. What would be the public reaction to the headline: "Boston Strangler Clears Cambridge Mugger"? Is that more shocking than: "Attica Massacre Chief Clears Assassination Plotters"?

Rockefeller was the perfect choice to head a commission investigating the CIA. Questioned during his nomination hearing last fall by Sen. Hatfield: "Do you believe that the Central Intelligence Agency should ever actively participate in the internal affairs of another sovereign country, such as in the case of Chile?" Rockefeller replied, "I assume they were done in the best national interest."

According to CIA head William Colby's testimony, the CIA tried—with $8 million—to change the election results in Chile when it seemed a Marxist, Allende, would win. American corporations didn't like Allende because he stood for nationalization of Anaconda Copper and other businesses. Anaconda Copper owed a quarter of a billion dollars to a group of banks led by Chase Manhattan, whose chairman is David Rockefeller, Nelson's brother. Now we are catching on to the meaning of "national interest."

But the circle is still not closed. The CIA action to overthrow Allende was approved by the Forty Committee, whose chairman is Henry Kissinger. And it was Kissinger who recommended that Rockefeller head the commission to investigate the CIA.

Rockefeller summed up the commission report: "There are things that have been done which are in contradiction to the statutes, but in comparison to the total effort, they are not major."

The same report can be made on the Corleone family, after studying them in the motion picture *The Godfather*. True, they murdered people who challenged their power, but in comparison to all the harmless things they did, like drinking espresso, going to weddings and christenings, and bouncing grandchildren on their knees, it was nothing to get excited about.

Yes, the CIA had its little faults. For instance:

It kept secret files on 10,000 American citizens. It engaged in domestic wiretapping, breaking and entering, and opening people's mail. It approved Mr. Nixon's "dirty tricks" plan, and abetted Howard Hunt's burglarizing. All this was illegal. And its director, Richard Helms, lied about it to the Senate Foreign Relations Committee.

The CIA plotted to overthrow various governments: successfully in Iran and Guatemala, unsuccessfully in Cuba. It discussed assassinating Fidel Castro, with the Kennedys' approval, Gen. Lansdale has testified.

The CIA ran a program of assassination, torture, and imprisonment in Vietnam between 1967 and 1971, called Operation Phoenix, headed by the present CIA director William Colby, who admitted over 20,000 Vietnamese civilians were executed without trial. That is a bloodbath, by any definition.

One more fact: no President, no Congress, no Supreme Court, for 25 years, has done anything to stop these activities.

There is murder and deceit on the record of the CIA. But we mustn't abolish it, because we need it to fight Communism. Why do we need to fight Communism? Because Communism roams the earth, conspiring to overthrow other governments. And because we don't want to live in a society where secret police tap our wires, open our mail, and have the power to quietly eliminate anyone they decide will hurt "national security." Once, there was the Stone Age. Now, the Age of Irony.

It is only fitting that Rockefeller and his commission should befriend the CIA. It would confuse us if they denounced members of their own club. The Rockefeller report clears the air; our problem is not the CIA, but the club itself.

10

The Curious Chronology
of the Mayaguez Incident

In April of 1975, Secretary of State Henry Kissinger was quoted in the *Washington Post* as follows: "The U.S. must carry out some act somewhere in the world which shows its determination to continue to be a world power." The following month came the "Mayaguez Incident." The Mayaguez was an American cargo ship sailing from South Vietnam to Thailand in mid-May 1975, just three weeks after the defeat of the United States in Vietnam. When it came close to an island in Cambodia, where a revolutionary regime had just taken power, the ship was stopped by the Cambodians, taken to a port at a nearby island, and the crew removed to the mainland. President Ford demanded the release of the crew, and when thirty-six hours passed without their release (though it was not clear his demand had been received by the Cambodians), he began military operations. It was bizarre that the United States should use this situation to try to re-establish its reputation as the foremost military power in the world. As a columnist for the *Boston Globe* at this time, I wrote the following piece, which appeared in the May 23, 1975 issue.

I t was a small incident, they say. Restraint was used. No B52s. Only 15 or 18 of our men died, by gunfire or drowning. Add 23 killed in a hushed-up helicopter crash over Thailand. Only 50 wounded.

So the Mayaguez affair is hardly worth mentioning. Unless, as some think, every human life is precious.

Let us agree first, the Cambodians did not behave wisely. It is unwise to take even a single marble from the neighborhood bully—he might smash your head in. And even if you bloody his nose a bit, he will prance all over the block, claiming a huge victory, confident now that no others will dare steal a marble, since they might have an eye gouged out just to teach them a lesson.

The Cambodians were unwise. But courteous. "A man who spoke English greeted us with a handshake and welcomed us to Cambodia," the crew said. "Capt. Miller and his men all said they were never abused by the captors. There were even accounts of kind treatment—of Cambodian soldiers feeding them first and eating what the Americans left, of the soldiers giving the seamen the mattresses off their beds." So reported the press.

The Cambodians asked the crew about spying and the CIA. Absurd questions of course; we never spy, and the CIA is a research group. Apparently persuaded of the ship's innocent intent after a half-day's discussion, they agreed to release the crew, and put them on a fishing boat headed for the American fleet (about 6:15 P.M., Wednesday, May 14, our time). At 7 P.M., Phnom Penh radio, heard in Bangkok, announced release of the Mayaguez.

Meanwhile, the American government, with no evidence that the men were being harmed, with no indication that the Cambodians had rejected or even received its messages, not waiting even 48 hours to work things out peacefully (the crew was detained early Monday morning; by Tuesday evening we were bombing ships), began military operations.

The chronology of those operations is curious, as one pieces it together:

Curiosity No. 1: On Tuesday evening, the boat taking the crew from Tang Island to the mainland had been flown over and strafed by American jets in such a way as to indicate they knew the crew was aboard. Indeed, President Ford told the Senate that crewmen were thought to be on a boat that left Tang. Yet, Wednesday afternoon, Mr. Ford ordered an attack on Tang Island.

Curiosity No. 2: The marine assault on Tang Island began about 7:15 P.M. Wednesday. But an hour earlier, the crewmen had already been released by the Cambodians and were on their way back. They were sighted at 10:45 P.M. and the captain said it was a four and a half hour trip, so they must have started out around 6:15 P.M. Furthermore, a U.S. recon plane circled and signaled that it had spotted them. Surely it would then have radioed headquarters. Then why the attack on Tang, with all the ensuing dead and wounded?

Curiosity No. 3: Why, with crew and ship recovered, did U.S. planes bomb the Cambodian mainland, twice? To protect Marines still on Tang? With total sea and air control, the United States could easily have intercepted any Cambodian force moving towards Tang.

The New York Times talked about the "admirable efficiency" of the operation. Efficient? It was a military disaster: Five of 11 helicopters, in the invasion force blown up or disabled, and no provision made for replacements to lift Marines off the island. One-third of the landing force was soon dead or wounded (65 out of 200). That exceeds the casualty rate in the World War II invasion of Iwo Jima.

How to explain all this? Blundering? Addiction in Washington to violent solutions? A brutal disregard of Cambodian and American lives to score points for Mr. Ford's nomination and Kissinger's prestige? The "tin, rubber, and oil" listed in the Pentagon Papers to explain U.S. interest in Southeast Asia? Or all of the above?

11

Dow Shalt Not Kill

The protest against the war took many forms. Violence was rare, engaged in by a small number of individuals on the fringe of the movement and generally disapproved by the movement as a whole. The general spirit of the movement was to follow the lead of the civil rights movement, to base its actions on the principle of non-violent direct action. This often meant confrontations with authority on many levels, including blocking streets and corporate offices, invading draft boards and destroying draft records (destruction of property, especially property that was an instrument of war, was not, unlike action against people, considered an act of violence). For instance, there were many demonstrations in Minneapolis against Minneapolis-Honeywell Corporation, which was manufacturing "cluster bombs," deadly packages of exploding pellets which left machines untouched, but people—mostly civilians—severely wounded and in agony. There were liberals who were made nervous by acts of trespassing, blockading, obstruction, arguing that they constituted violations of civil liberties. I did not think so, and used the occasion of a demonstration in which I participated, against the Dow Chemical Company, manufacturer of the deadly napalm, to make an argument defending such actions on both constitutional and moral grounds. My essay appeared in the *New South Student* in December 1967, and was reprinted in a number of other periodicals.

M any faculty members and students, being passionate opponents of American violence in Vietnam, and also insistent civil libertarians, are troubled by the recent demonstrations against Dow Chemical. No dilemma exists where the action is merely protest—by picketing, leafleting, speaking—against Dow, napalm, and the war. That is a plain exercise of free speech, press, and assembly.

But physical interposition, where Dow recruiters are blocked from carrying on their recruiting, opens puzzling questions. As one concerned both with civil liberties and the war, I would like to think aloud for a while, in print, and try to reach some conclusions.

First, it seems to me that the "civil liberties" of Dow Chemical are not in question. "Civil liberties" encompass various forms of freedom of expression, as well as certain procedural guarantees against arbitrary police or judicial action, and are fairly well covered by the First, Eighth, and Fourteenth Amendments. No one is abrogating Dow's right to express its views: indeed, the recent demonstrators in this area invited the Dow representative to state his case publicly, and gave him a platform for this purpose. If Dow wanted to set up a table, or hold a meeting, to declare its views, any interference would be a violation of civil liberties.

However, the *actions* of an individual or group which (unlike even the most malicious or slanderous speech) have immediate and irremediable effects on the lives and liberties of others, must sometimes be restricted for the health and safety of the public. Thus, we pass laws against murder, rape, arson. Thus, we regulate the sale and manufacture of harmful products. We even restrict the restaurant owner's freedom to choose his customers by racial standards. To put it more broadly: the whole body of criminal and social legislation is designed to restrict some people's freedom of action (not their civil liberties) in order to safeguard the health and happiness of others. Therefore, a *law* which prevented

Dow Chemical Company from recruiting people who might be engaged in the manufacture, sale or promotion of a substance to be dropped on men, women, and children in order to burn them to death would be easily as justifiable as the Meat Inspection Act of 1906. It would (unlike a law interfering with talk for or against such a substance) no more be an infringement of civil liberties than a law barring the indiscriminate sale of deadly poisons at the corner grocery.

Robber Barons

The doctrine that the "civil liberties" of corporations are violated by regulatory laws was predominant in this country during the age of the "Robber Barons," and was constitutionally sanctioned for about fifty years, until 1938. Then, a sharply-worded opinion by Justice Black (*Connecticut General Life Insurance Co. v. Johnson*) declared that corporations should no longer be considered "persons" to be protected by the due process clause of the 14th Amendment. It soon became established in constitutional law that the regulation of business was not a deprivation of a civil liberty, that what is known as "substantive due process" would apply only to cases where real persons were being deprived of their rights of free expression. Today, it is well-established constitutionally that the U.S. government could make illegal the manufacture of napalm, and charge any persons recruiting for a napalm-manufacturing company with conspiring to violate the law.

But: there is no such law. Indeed, the government itself has ordered the napalm manufactured by Dow, and is using it to burn and kill Vietnamese peasants. Should private citizens (students and faculty—in this instance) act themselves, by physical interposition, against Dow Chemical's business activities?

To do so would be to "take the law into your own hands." That is exactly what civil disobedience is: the temporary taking of the law into one's own hands, in order to declare what the law *should* be. It is a declaration that there is an incongruence between the law and humane values, and that sometimes this can only be publicized by breaking the law.

Civil disobedience can take two forms: violating a law which is obnoxious; or symbolically enacting a law which is urgently needed. When Negroes sat-in at lunch counters, they were engaging in both forms: they violated state laws on segregation and trespassing; they were also symbolically enacting a public accommodations law even before it was written into the Civil Rights Act of 1964.

Most of us, I assume, would support civil disobedience under *some* circumstances: we would commend those who defied the Fugitive Slave Act by harboring a Negro slave, and those who symbolically enacted emancipation by trying to prevent soldiers in Boston from returning Anthony Burns to his master. Otherwise, to declare that the law in *all* circumstances is to be obeyed, is to suppress the very spirit of democracy, to surrender individual conscience to an omnipotent state. Thus, the issue becomes: under what circumstances is civil disobedience justified and is the Dow Chemical situation one of those circumstances?

It seems to me there are two essential conditions for the right to civil disobedience. One is that the human value at stake must involve fundamental rights, like life, health, and liberty. There is no real cause, for instance, to disobey a traffic light because it is inconveniently long. But human slavery, or racism, or war—these are overwhelmingly important. Thus, the argument "what if everyone disobeyed the law every time it displeased them" falls before the observable fact that those who engage in civil disobedience are almost always law-abiding citizens who on certain very important issues deliberately, openly, temporarily violate the law to communicate a vital message to their fellow citizens.

What of Dow Chemical and napalm? Four American physicians, in a report, "Medical Problems of South Vietnam," have written: "Napalm is a highly sticky inflammable jelly which clings to anything it touches and burns with such heat that all oxygen in the area is exhausted within moments. Death is either by roasting or by suffocation. Napalm wounds are often fatal (estimates are 90 percent). Those who survive face a living death. The victims are frequently children." Napalm is dropped daily on the villages, the forests, the people of Vietnam by American bombers; the

saturation bombing of that tiny country is one of the cruelest acts perpetrated by any nation in modern history; it ranks with the destruction of
Lidice by the Germans, the crushing of the Hungarian rebellion by the
Russians, or the recent mass slaughter in Indonesia. Dr. Richard E. Perry,
an American physician, wrote in *Redbook* in January 1967, on his return
from Vietnam: "I have been an orthopedic surgeon for a good number of
years, with rather a wide range of medical experience. But nothing could
have prepared me for my encounters with Vietnamese women and children burned by napalm. It was shocking and sickening, even for a physician, to see and smell the blackened flesh."

We are not, then, dealing with trivialities, but with monstrous deeds.
This fact somehow becomes lost in the bland, reasoned talk of business-
men and university officials, who speak as if Dow were just another business firm, recruiting for some innocuous purpose, making radios or
toothpaste.

The root issue, it should be clear, is not simply napalm; it is the
Vietnam war as a whole, in which a far-off country is being systematical-
ly destroyed, and its population decimated, by the greatest military power
on earth. The war itself is the object of the civil disobedience; the use of
napalm is one particularly bestial tactic in this war.

This brings us to the second condition for civil disobedience: the
inadequacy of legal channels for redressing the grievance. This is mani-
festly true in the case of the Vietnam war, which is being waged completely outside the American constitutional process, by the President and
a handful of advisers. Congress is troubled, but follows sheep-like what
the White House decrees. The Supreme Court, by tradition, leaves foreign policy questions to the "political" branches of government (the
President and Congress) but recently one of its more conservative members, Justice Potter Stewart, said that perhaps the Court should review the
constitutionality of the war. This, after 100,000 American casualties!
Citizens have taken to the auditoriums and to the streets precisely
because they have no other way to protest; yet both President and Vice-
President declare with the brazenness of petty dictators that no civic out-

cry will change their policy. If ever there was an issue which called for civil disobedience, it is this run-away war.

Then why do we become uneasy when students interfere with Dow Chemical? Occasionally, we read of housewives blocking off a busy intersection because children have been killed there as a result of a lack of traffic lights. These housewives thereby interfere with the freedom of automobiles and of pedestrians, in order to temporarily regulate, or even disrupt, traffic, on behalf of the lives of children—hoping this will lead to the permanent regulation of traffic by government. (Those are not *the* automobiles that killed the child, anymore than *this* Dow Chemical representative, or the student he is recruiting, is actually dropping the napalm bomb.)

Why do we so easily sympathize with actions like that, where perhaps one child was killed, and not with actions against Dow Chemical, where countless children have been victims? Is it possible that we subconsciously distinguish between the identifiable children down the street (who move us), and the faceless children of that remote Asian land (who do not)? It is possible also that the well-dressed, harassed representative of Dow Chemical is more human, therefore more an object of sympathy, to the well-dressed, harassed officials of the University (and to us), than the burning, bleeding, blurred faces of the Vietnamese?

There is a common argument which says: but where will these student actions lead? If we justify one act of civil disobedience, must we not justify them all? Do they then have a right to disobey the Civil Rights Acts? Where does it stop? That argument withers away, however, once we recognize the distinction between free speech, where absolute toleration is a social good, and free action, where the existence of values other than free speech demands that we *choose* right over wrong—and respond accordingly. We should remember that the social utility of free speech is in giving us the informational base from which we can then make social choices. To refrain from making choices is to say that beyond the issue of free speech we have no substantive values which we will express in action. If we do not discriminate in the actions we support or oppose, we cannot rectify the terrible injustices of the present world.

Whether the issue of the Vietnam war is more effectively presented by protest and demonstration (that is, the exercise of speech, press, assembly) rather than by civil disobedience, is a question of tactic, and varies with each specific situation. Different student groups (at Harvard and MIT, for instance) have used one or another against Dow recruitment, and each tactic has its own advantages. I tend to favor the protest tactic as keeping the central issue of the war clearer. But, if students or faculty engaged in civil disobedience, I would consider that morally defensible.

So much for student-faculty action—but what of the University administration? The University's acceptance of Dow Chemical recruiting as just another business transaction is especially disheartening, because it is the University which tells students repeatedly on ceremonial occasions that it hopes students will be more than fact-absorbing automatons, that they will choose humane values, and stand up for them courageously. For the University to sponsor Dow Chemical activities as a protective civil liberty means that the University (despite its courses in Constitutional Law) still accepts the nineteenth century definition of substantive due process as defending corporations against regulation, that (despite a library with books on civil liberties) the University still does not understand what civil liberties are, that (despite its entrance requirement of literacy) the University has not read in the newspapers of the terrible damage our napalm bombs have done to innocent people.

The fact that there is only an indirect connection between Dow recruiting students and napalm dropped on Vietnamese villages, does not vitiate the moral issue. It is precisely the nature of modern mass murder that it is not visibly direct like individual murder, but takes on a corporate character, where every participant has limited liability. The total effect, however, is a thousand times more pernicious, than that of the individual entrepreneur of violence. If the world is destroyed, it will be a white-collar crime, done in a business-like way, by large numbers of individuals involved in a chain of actions, each one having a touch of innocence.

Sometimes the University speaks of the "right of recruitment." There is no absolute right of recruitment, however, because (beyond the package of civil liberties connected with free expression and procedural guarantees, which are the closest we can get to "absolute" right) all rights are relative. I doubt that Boston University would open its offices to the Ku Klux Klan for recruiting, or that it would apply an absolute right of private enterprise to peddlers selling poisonous food on campus. When the University of Pennsylvania announced it would end its germ-warfare research project, it was saying that there is no absolute right to do research on *anything*, for *any* purpose.

The existence of University "security" men (once known as campus police) testifies that all actions on campus are not equally tolerable. The University makes moral choices all the time. If it can regulate the movement of men into women's dormitories (in a firm stand for chastity), then why cannot it regulate the coming and going of corporations into the university, where the value is human life, and the issue is human suffering?

And if students are willing to take the risks of civil disobedience, to declare themselves for the dying people of Vietnam, cannot the University take a milder step, but one which makes the same declaration—and cancel the invitation to Dow Chemcal? Why cannot the University—so much more secure—show a measure of social commitment, a bit of moral courage? Should not the University, which speaks so often about students having "values," declare some of its own? It is written on no tablets handed down from heaven that the officials of a University may not express themselves on public issues. It is time (if not now, when? asks the Old Testament) for a University to forsake the neutrality of the IBM machines, and join the human race.

12

A Speech for LBJ

It is a common occurrence in American politics that critics of a
certain policy, while fervently declaring their allegiance to
moral principle, nevertheless say they can "understand" the
reluctance of the President to act on such principle because of
the "realities" of politics, that he cannot "afford" (a word I
always associated with dire poverty and not with the occupant
of the White House) to go against "public opinion." This is
almost always a feeble rationalization for a deep lack of principle, and when the same argument for "realism" was put
forth against the idea of withdrawal from Vietnam, I decided
to challenge it. It seemed to me that public opinion was usually ahead of the national government on moral issues, that in
any case such opinion was extremely volatile and movable by
reasonable argument. My method was to write a speech for
Lyndon Johnson which would persuasively explain to
Americans more than ready for such an explanation, indeed
eager for it as the bodybags of their sons were returning home
in great numbers, why he was immediately withdrawing our
military machine from Vietnam. I ended my book *Vietnam: The
Logic of Withdrawal* with that speech. A businessman bought
six hundred copies of the book and sent it to every member of

Congress. The speech was reprinted in full-page ads in news-papers in various parts of the country. The *Cleveland Plain Dealer* ran simultaneous articles by Congressman Mendel Rivers of South Carolina, urging escalation of the war, by Senator William Fulbright, calling for gradual de-escalation and negoti-ations, and by me, agruing for immediate withdrawal. The paper then took a poll of its readers and 63 percent voted for immediate withdrawal. A columnist for the *Plain Dealer* wrote: "Howard Zinn, a professor of government at Boston University, who served as a bombardier in World War II, has written a speech for Lyndon Johnson which, if he delivered it, would make the President one of the great men of history in my opin-ion." But Johnson did not deliver that speech. He did start negotiations with the Vietnamese in Paris, and announced he would not run for President in 1968. The war continued, and the anti-war movement grew, and in 1973 the United States finally withdrew; 55,000 Americans had lost their lives, Vietnam was devastated, and two million of its people, mostly civilians, were dead. Here is the speech I wrote in 1967.

M y Fellow Americans:

Not long ago I received a letter from my fourth-grade school teacher who still lives back in the little town where I grew up. She is of advanced age now, but still as she was when I sat in her class, a kindly and wise woman. She had been through depression and war, through sickness and the death of loved ones, more than most of us. Let me share her letter with you; I am sure she will not mind.

> Dear Lyndon: You know I have always had faith in you and knew you would do what is right. And you have been trying your best on this Vietnam situation. But nothing seems to be going right. So many people are getting killed. Not only our boys, but all those poor people over there.

You have tried talking peace. And you have tried bombing, and what not. But there is no end in sight. I hear people in town saying: "We should never have gotten in, but now that we are in, we don't seem able to get out." Lyndon, can't you get us out? I am getting on now in years and would like to see peace again. God bless you. Sincerely, Mrs. Annie Mae Lindley

Now let me read just one more letter to you. It came to me from a young man fighting with the First Marine Division in South Vietnam:

Dear Mr. President: I am twenty years old and enlisted in the Marines as soon as I left high school in Massilon, Ohio. I have been in Vietnam six months now, and I have seen a lot. Three days ago my closest buddy was killed. Yesterday our outfit destroyed a hamlet that Intelligence said had been used by the VC as a base. We burned the huts and threw grenades down the tunnels. But there were no VC there. In one of the tunnels there were two women and three kids. We didn't know that. One of the kids was killed and one of the women lost an eye. We rounded up all the villagers and they stood around—children, old folks, women—crying and afraid. Of course we didn't mean to kill any kids. But we did. And that's war. I know you need sometimes to do nasty things for an important cause. The trouble is—there doesn't seem much of a cause left here in Vietnam. We're supposed to be defending these people against the VC. But they don't want us to defend them. They don't care about Communism or politics or anything like that. They just want to be left in peace. So, more and more, my buddies and I wonder—what are we doing here? We're not afraid. We've been sticking it out, in the mud and in the jungle. And we'll go on like this if you ask us to. But somehow it seems wrong. I don't know what we should do, but I just thought I'd let you know how some of us feel. Sincerely, James Dixon, Corporal 1st Marine Division.

My fellow Americans, let me tell you, I have read and reread these two letters, and they have been on my mind. You all know how my administration has been concerned with the war in Vietnam. Night after night I have sat up thinking, and sometimes—I don't mind telling you—praying, that we would find a way to end this terrible war, which has cost tens of thousands of lives, American and Vietnamese, and which has caused so much pain and suffering to millions of people in that unfortunate little country.

What have been our objectives in Vietnam? I have said many times that what we wanted was for Vietnam to be free to determine its own affairs—that this is why we were fighting. We have tried every possible way to gain this objective. We have offered negotiations. And we have fought—hard, and courageously, on unfamiliar territory—with an increasing commitment of planes, ships and ground forces, all designed to bring the war to an end with honor.

I don't need to tell you that we have not been successful. We have not destroyed the Vietcong's will to fight. This is not a pleasant fact to report, but it is a fact.

There is another unpleasant fact to report. The government we have been supporting in Vietnam has not succeeded in gaining the respect of its own people there. No matter how valiant our men are, they cannot fight a war that is not supported by the people of the country we committed ourselves to defend. Always implied in our commitment was that if the war threatened to become our war, rather than a war by and for the Vietnamese, we would reconsider our position. That time has now come.

We have tried force, and we have offered negotiations. Neither has worked. Some have criticized us for not trying even more force. Of course we could do this. No one in the world needs to be told how powerful we are. We can stay in Vietnam as long as we like. We can reduce the whole country to ashes. We are powerful enough to do this. But we are not cruel enough to do this. I, as your president, am not willing to engage in a war without end that would destroy the youth of this nation and the people of Vietnam.

We had hoped this war could end by negotiations. But this has not worked. Pride and self-respect have often stood in the way for both sides. We are not willing to beg for negotiations. And we have too much compassion for those dying each day in Vietnam to let the war continue. In Korea, you may remember, the war dragged on, while the negotiators tried to agree on terms. The diplomats talked, while men died. For two years they talked, and for two years the corpses piled up in that unfortunate land. We do not want that kind of negotiation in Vietnam.

The American people have the courage to fight. We have shown this a dozen times in the past, from Bunker Hill to Gettysburg, from Normandy to Guadalcanal. We also have the courage to stop fighting, not when someone else decides for us, but when we decide for ourselves.

As commander-in-chief of the armed forces, I have ordered that, as of midnight tonight, our Air Force and our Navy will halt the bombings in North and South Vietnam. We have not run out of planes, nor have we run out of bombs, nor have we run out of the determination to use them when it is wise. What we have run out of is the willingness to see more people die under our bombs. Too many have died. Too many have suffered. It is time to call a halt.

Also, I have given orders to General Westmoreland, the capable and courageous Commander of our forces in Vietnam, to halt offensive operations and to begin the orderly withdrawal of our armed forces from that country.

Let us speak frankly now about the consequences of this decision.

We may see a period of turmoil and conflict in Vietnam. But that was true before we arrived. That is the nature of the world. It is hard to imagine, however, any conflict that will be more destructive than what is going on now. Our departure will inevitably diminish the fighting. It may end it.

There are many places in the world where people are going through the disorder and the violence of social change. The United States cannot interfere in every one of those instances. We do not intend to do so. To the extent that the United Nations can mediate in helping to bring tranquility to Vietnam, we will happily lend our moral and financial support.

Vietnam may become a Communist nation. The northern half of that country has been Communist for some time, and a good part of the population in the South has been sympathetic to the Vietcong. Desperate people often turn to Communism. But we have shown that we can live in peace with Communist nations, if there is mutual respect. Despite our many disagreements, we have maintained peaceful relations with the

Soviet Union, with Yugoslavia, with Poland, with other Communist nations. We can certainly live in peace with Vietnam.

Everyone knows that behind our military activity in Vietnam has been our concern that Communist China shall not press its weght on other countries. Many experts on China have told us that much of China's belligerent attitude has been due to nationalistic feeling and to her fear that we intend to attack her. I hereby give my pledge that the United States will never initiate a war with China, and we will begin soon to seek ways and means of coming to a more amicable relationshp with her.

I have often said that the most effective means of maintaining a free society does not consist of armed might, but of economic development and prosperity. That will be our aim now in Asia.

To this end, I am going to ask Congress to take half of the $20 billion allocated for the Vietnam War this year and to put it into a fund— an international fund, if the United Nations will set this up—for the economic development of Vietnam and other countries in Southeast Asia. We will not force our favors upon these countries. But we will stand ready to help—with no political strings attached—on the basis of their own declarations, their own needs.

The war in Vietnam was beginnng to slow down many of our plans for the Great Society—plans to end poverty, to build homes and schools, to rebuild our cities, to eliminate the slums which have been at the root of unrest in various parts of the country. There will be $10 billion left unused from the war. I will ask Congress to redirect that money for purposes which I will outline in a special message next week.

We have made an important decision. It is a decision based on a fundamental American belief that human life is sacred, that peace is precious, and that true power does not consist in the brute force of guns and bombs, but in the economic well-being of a free people.

The dream I have always had since I was a boy in Texas, I still have— and I want to fulfill it for America. We are about to embark on a venture far more glorious, far more bold, requiring far more courage—than war. Our aim is to build a society which will set an example for the rest of mankind. I am happy to stand before you tonight and to say that we will now build this Great Society in earnest.

I need not tell you how long I have waited for this moment—and how happy I am to be able to say that now, after so much pain, after so much sacrifice, our boys will be coming home.

My fellow Americans, good night and sleep well. We are no longer at war in Vietnam.

13

Of Fish and Fishermen

In June of 1966, I was invited to Japan, along with Ralph Featherstone, a black SNCC worker I knew from Mississippi. Our hosts were members of Beheiren, a Japanese group organized around opposition to the American war in Vietnam—they were journalists, novelists, poets, philosophers, movie-makers. Ralph and I traveled north to south through Japan, from Hokkaido to Hiroshima and Fukuoka, and across the East China Sea to Okinawa. We spoke at fourteen universities in nine different cities, at big meetings and small ones, at tea gatherings and beer sessions, with trade unionists and housewives. We found them virtually unanimous in their belief that the United States policy in Vietnam was not just a bit awry, but profoundly wrong. When I returned, wanting people in the United States to get a Japanese perspective on the war, I wrote an article for *Ramparts* magazine, which appeared in 1967 under the title "Of Fish and Fishermen," and then, in another form, as a chapter in *Vietnam: The Logic of Withdrawal.* (A tragic note: not long after our return from Japan, my companion on that trip, Ralph Featherstone, newly married, still involved with SNCC and the Movement, was killed when a bomb of unknown origin exploded in a car he was driving.)

There is an eerie ten minute motion picture called *The Fisherman*, in which a happy American angler hauls sleek, fat leaping fish out of the ocean and piles them lifeless on the beach, meanwhile devouring candy bars from his lunchbox. He finally runs out of food. Restless, unhappy, he sees a paper sack nearby with a sandwich in it, bites into the sandwich, and is hooked. He digs his feet frantically into the sand, but he is dragged, twisting and struggling at the end of a line, into the sea. The effect on the viewer is a sudden reverse of perspective, both horrifying and healthful, in which, for the first time he sees himself, the Fisherman, from the standpoint of the Fish.

Something like that happens when you spend time in Japan talking to the Japanese about American policy in Vietnam. The brutality of the war we are waging, no matter how sharply we feel it on occasion, has the quality of fiction as it appears on television screens or in news columns. Always at hand to "explain" the bombing of villages, the death toll of civilians, the crushing of Buddhist dissidents, are earnest "liberals" (Humphrey and Goldberg), "realistic" experts (Rostow), genial spokesmen for the Administration (Rusk and McNamara). We listen with the languor of a people who have never been bombed, who have only been the bombardiers. So even our flickers of protest somehow end up muted and polite.

The Japanese have had a more intimate association with death, both as killers and as victims. We in America still cling to the romance of war that is not really war, but Terry and the Pirates, Defending the Free World, or LBJ in a Green Beret. For the Japanese, the recollection of themselves as kamikaze pilots, and then the turn-about-Hiroshima and Nagasaki, wore off all the sheen. Out of their experience, the Japanese want desperately to speak to us.

In Tokyo, rain cascading down outside, the auditorium at Meiji University filled, popular novelist Kaiko Ken told about his four months of note-taking on the front lines in Vietnam, much of the time spent with American soldiers. Kaiko, who is thirty-six, wore a sporty tan suit with open shirt collar, and tan suede shoes. "It used to be said in Vietnam that it is disastrous to be born a man, for you are drafted and killed; it is better to be a woman. But in South Vietnam today, a woman has a child at each side and one in her belly, and still must flee the American bombs." He had seen it himself, he said, that the Americans could not distinguish the Viet Cong from the air—no matter what the official assurances were—so they simply killed whomever they could find in the target area.

If this talk had been given in the United States, in any large gathering of students, one or more would have risen at some point in the discussion to challenge Kaiko's accusation—either to deny it, or to explain why the bombings were needed. In Japan, it is hard to find any defenders of American policy.

It was Kaiko, not a very political person, who last year collected money throughout Japan for a full-page ad which appeared in *The New York Times* as a plea to Americans: "The Japanese learned a bitter lesson from fifteen years of fighting on the Chinese mainland: weapons alone are of no avail in winning the minds and allegiance of any people. America's conduct of the war in Vietnam is alienating the sympathy of the Japanese." Corroboration of this last statement came from a journalist of long experience with a leading conservative newspaper in Japan, who said to me: "The polls show 80 percent of the Japanese opposed to U.S. policy in Vietnam. Emotionally, it is closer to 100 percent."

This was confirmed again and again as we talked with Japanese students and professors in 14 different universities along the 1,500 mile journey from Hokkaido to Okinawa. In Kyoto, a pediatrician spoke up from the audience. (Our interpreter—a poet and former Fulbright scholar in America—explained who the speaker was: "Dr. Matsuda's books on child care have sold in the millions; he is known as the Benjamin Spock of Japan.") Matsuda said: "What the United States does not understand is that communism is one of the effective ways in which underdeveloped countries become organized. Its reaction to this phenomenon in the world is neurotic." Matsuda, a vigorous man in his fifties, added: "Perhaps it needs..." Our interpreter hesitated at this point, and then translated the ending as "...a laxative." Then he corrected himself: "...a sedative."

At that meeting in Kyoto, a mountain-rimmed city of temples and pagodas, over a thousand people—students, faculty, town residents— came to talk about Vietnam. A ninety-two-year-old man, dean of the Buddhist priests in this holy city, spoke: "The American concept of free- dom violates the principles of self-determination. It is the kind of liber- alism that expresses only the purpose of the American state." And a Zen Buddhist, head shaven, in black robes and white scarf, said, "There is a major law in Buddhism—not to kill. Mass killing should not go on; that is the simple slogan that binds Japanese Buddhists with Buddhists in North and South Vietnam. And this should be brought to America."

It was in Kyoto that a young professor of astronomy spoke, with great feeling: "As a child, I was machine-gunned by an American plane. And at that moment there came a shock of realization that it was a human being who pulled the trigger. I wanted so much to have been able to say to him 'Please—don't pull the trigger!'"

You find many men in Japanese universities who spent time in jail for opposing Japanese aggression in the '30s. At Nagoya—sprawling, smoky, the Detroit of Japan—we were met by Professor Shinmura, who in 1936-37 put out a humanist magazine called *Sekai Bunka* (World Culture) until he was seized by the police. Shinmura, quiet, gray-haired with a slight stoop, is a specialist in French literature, and after release from prison made a living by anonymously translating the writings of Rolland, Diderot and others. I asked how many members of his faculty supported American policy in Vietnam. There were 600 on the faculty, including graduate asistants. No one knew of any who supported American policy.

To the Japanese we met, America was so clearly in the wrong, that it was incomprehensible to them why anyone believed Johnson and his cab- inet members. "No country should be permitted—as the U.S. is doing—

to smuggle counter-revolution to another country," a professor of literature at Hosei University in Tokyo said.

After a four hour discussion session at Tohoku University in Sendai,
a quiet town in northern Honshu, I was met by fifty students waiting
eagerly to continue the discussion. We trooped off to the park. There in
the cool darkness of Sendai, I wondered why fifty Japanese kids would
stay out after midnight to discuss the war in Vietnam, when Japan was
only a minor accessory to American action. When the U.S. was helping
the French crush the Algerian revolt, did any group of American students
ever gather in the park at midnight to brood over this? Did a thousand
ever meet to protest it? By the end of our trip I thought I had found the
answer. It lay in the Japanese people's piercing consciousness of their own
recent history. Again and again, at virtually every meeting, there arose the
accusation, directed at the Japanese past and the American present: "You
are behaving in Asia as we once did."

There is widespread and vocal recognition of Japan's own sins, from
the Manchurian invasion of 1931, to Pearl Harbor. Japanese scholars
have done much research on those years, and see in American actions in
Vietnam many of the same characteristics displayed by Japan in the '30s.
Unlike the Nazis, the Japanese did not abruptly replace parliamentary
democracy with authoritarian dictatorship. Rather, there was an almost
imperceptible growth of the power of the military within the outwardly
parliamentary system. When the Japanese took Manchuria in 1931,
then attacked China proper in 1937 and moved into Southeast Asia in
1940, they did not crassly declaim of world conquest like Hitler, but
spoke of a "co-prosperity sphere" which they were creating in Asia for
the benefit of all.

I asked one of Japan's most disginguished scholars about this analogy.
This was Professor Maruyama of Tokyo University, a political scientist and
prolific author, who five years ago was a visiting professor at Harvard.

"There are many differences," Maruyama said, "but one crucial element is
quite the same: the apologies and justification created by both govern-

ments for what is basically an attempt by a strong nation to establish a base of power inside a weaker one. Both Japan and the U.S. had difficulties and made excuses. The U.S. blames its difficulties in winning the Vietnamese war on China and North Vietnam. Japan attributed her failures not to the stubborn resistance of the Chinese, but to the aid of Great Britain and the United States. Japan declared that its aim was to emancipate the people of Southeast Asia and to bring them economic development. Just as the U.S. speaks not about economic and social reform while it carries on an essentially military action in Vietnam."

American commentators have a habit of dismissing Japanese criticism of our foreign policy as the work of communists, or—more vaguely—"leftists." This is comforting at first, but not after one reflects that most public opinion in the world, even in countries allied to us, is to the left of ours. We have become, since that period when Europe's monarchs feared we would spread the doctrine of revolution everywhere, a conservative nation. Even our "liberals" are conservative by global standards. Professor Maruyama said: "I am a liberal, not a radical. So I am concerned with what liberals in the States are doing. And I am very disappointed."

Our companions and interpreters in Japan were young intellectuals— two journalists, three novelists, a film producer, a poet, a philosopher— who last year decided to cross the maze of radical party lines in Japan and form a group (called Beheiren) dedicated to ending the war in Vietnam. Their chairman, Oda Makoto (family name first), is a wry thirty-four-year-old novelist who refuses to wear a tie no matter how formal the occasion. Oda started our meeting with students at Hokkaido University as follows: "You know, I got the idea for this tour of conscience while in the toilet. (Laughter) This is not strange. The peace movement starts like that, from the most common behavior of human life, from the elemental."

Oda, like most Japanese intellectuals, is critical of Communist China, but with no more heat than he is critical of Japan or America. He sees it as a new society, with the spit and fire that other new nations show, but not as a threat to the rest of Asia. It shows no signs of wanting to gobble up Southeast Asia; it maintains pacific relations with Burma—which is defenseless along a very long border—and with Cambodia. And, in contrast to the United States, China does not have a single soldier stationed outside its borders. Japanese intellectuals do not doubt that, in view of China's behavior, the U.S. is acting hysterically, and that people in Vietnam are dying unnecessarily because of it.

The United States keeps saying its aim is a free and prosperous Asia, but the Asians themselves, including the Vietnamese, are far from ardent about this war, and the only countries giving substantial aid to the American military effort (Korea and Thailand) are those which are economically dependent on the U.S., under its military occupation, and controlled by elites which can ignore popular desire. Japan is also a station for American troops (under the much-resented Security Treaty of 1960) and its former territory, Okinawa, has been taken away by the U.S. and converted into one of the most powerful military bases in the world. ("Please inform your fellow Americans," a Tokyo University student sociologist said, "that the majority of Japanese do not think these military bases protect Japan's security—in fact they feel endangered by them.") Nevertheless, the government of Premier Sato, while nodding and bowing to the U.S. Department of State, keeps a wary eye on the Japanese public, knowing their feelings.

Our envoy to Japan, Edwin Reischauer, an astute scholar of Asian affairs before his appointment, now lives in a comfortable bubble of his own in the Embassy, quietly ignoring Japanese disapproval of this country's actions. My last hour in Tokyo was spent in rapid-fire dialogue with him, trying to penetrate that bubble. But, except for Reischauer's personal charm, it was like listening to an LBJ press conference, or a McNamara briefing.

Reischauer thought differently in 1954 when, as a Harvard expert on Japan, he wrote *Wanted: An Asian Policy*. In it, he described the French suppression of the Viet Minh, with American aid, as "a sobering example of the weakness of defending the status quo." He found the main reason for the effectiveness of the Communists "in the realm of ideas" and because they "carried out much needed land reform for the peasants." He wishes the U.S. "had the foresight and the courage in the early postwar years to persuade the French to extricate themselves soon enough from their untenable position in Indochina." And, he said a policy based largely on stopping communism was "a dangerous oversimplification of our Asian problem." In his book, he accused American policy-makers of "frenzied emotionalism" and "dangerous inflexibility." But now he is the ambassador.

Japan is an embarrassment, because it was under our post-war tutelage that she put into her 1947 Constitution the statement: "...never again shall we be visited with the horrors of war through the action of government." And Article 9 contains a silent reproach to what the United States is doing in Vietnam: "...the Japanese people forever renounce war as a sovereign right of the nation and the threat or use of force as a means of settling international disputes." It is the old human story, the little boy nurtured by his family on the Biblical exhortation Thou Shalt Not Kill, watching his father return, gun still smoking from a mission of murder.

The Japanese are trying to speak to us, but we will not listen. They have been both Fish and Fisherman, in a short space of time. We in the United States have never had to struggle at the end of the hook—and lose. We have no Hiroshima, no city of the blind and maimed, no professors still haggard from long terms in jail. And while, on a number of occasions, we have been the Fisherman, we have never been forced, as the Japanese have, to recognize our deeds, to bow, to apologize, to promise a life of peace. We have, in other words, never been caught.

14

Vietnam: A Matter of Perspective

Those of us who had been involved in the Southern movement were not likely to accept, without deep suspicion, that the United States government—so loath to protect equal rights in its own country—was dropping bombs in Vietnam on behalf of democracy or liberty or self-determination or any other noble principle. In August 1964, the bodies of civil rights workers Chaney, Goodman and Schwerner were discovered in Neshoba County, Mississippi, shot to death. Earlier in the summer, a delegation of black Mississippians had traveled to Washington to plead with the national government for federal protection, and was received with silence. At a memorial service for the three young men, Bob Moses, SNCC organizer in Mississippi, held up a copy of that morning's newspaper which headlined LBJ SAYS SHOOT TO KILL IN THE GULF OF TONKIN. The United States had been conducting secret naval operations off the coast of North Vietnam and now claimed U.S. destroyers, on "routine patrol" had been fired on—a claim full of deceptions and outright lies, it turned out. Moses commented bitterly on the fact that the federal government refused protection for civil rights workers but was ready to send its armed forces halfway around the world for a cause no one could reasonably explain. I became involved in the anti-war movement very soon after that summer, spoke at the first anti-war rally on the Boston Common in the spring of 1965, and began writing about the war. In 1967 Beacon Press published my book *Vietnam: The Logic of Withdrawal,* which immediately went through eight printings. Reprinted here is the introductory chapter to that book.

Vietnam, it seems to me, has become a theater of the absurd. 1. By late 1966, the United States was spending for the Vietnam war at an annual rate of twenty billion dollars, enough to give every family in South Vietnam (whose normal annual income is not more than several hundred dollars) about $5,000 for the year. Our monthly expentiture for the war exceeds our annual expenditure for the Great Society's poverty program.

2. Early in 1966, a new pacification technique was developed by American soldiers. It involved surrounding a village, killing as many young men as could be found, and then taking away the women and children by helicopter. The Americans called this procedure "Operation County Fair."

3. The Pentagon disclosed in 1966 that it had paid to relatives an average of $34 in condolence money for each Vietnamese killed accidentally in American air strikes during that summer. At the same time, according to reports from Saigon, the Air Force was paying $87 for each rubber tree destroyed accidentally by bombs.

4. A *New York Times* dispatch from Saigon, June 21, 1966:

> The United States Air Force turned its attention yesterday to a column of 10 water buffalos sighted along a road just north of the Mugia Pass on the Laotian-North Vietnamese border.
>
> The spokesman said the buffalos were heavily laden with what was suspected to be enemy ammunition. The animals died under fire from

F105 Thunderchief jets. The spokesman said, "There were no secondary explosions."

United States Marine pilots also strafed a column of 11 pack elephants in the mountains 35 miles southwest of Danang in South Vietnam yesterday. Five of the animals were killed and five others seen to fall. Again there were no secondary explosions.

5. A Chicago newspaper, asked by a reader if it were true that for every enemy soldier it killed in Vietnam the United States was killing six civilians, replied that this was not true; we were killing only four civilians for every soldier.

6. Covering the Buddhist revolt against the Ky government in early 1966, *Life* magazine showed a photo of a South Vietnamese soldier coming up behind an unarmed, gowned Buddhist monk and clubbing him unconscious. No comment was made by *Life*.

7. At his press conference on March 22, 1966, at a time of expanding warfare and growing casualties in Vietnam, President Johnson said, among other things: "If I get real depressed when I read how everything has gone bad here, I just ask for the letters from Vietnam so I can cheer up."

8. The January 16, 1965 *Milwaukee Journal* reported that a young man who had studied agricultural economics at the University of Minnesota, learning to aid underdeveloped countries improve their yields, was now an Air Force captain and was using his knowledge to point out productive rice fields in Vietnam, so that United States planes could destroy them with bombs and chemicals.

9. In the spring of 1966, a journalist interviewed an Air Force general in Saigon:

> Journalist: Let me ask you a philosophical question. What is your reply to those who say we ought to stop our bombing—both North and South—and that would bring us closer to negotiating an end to this war?
> General: Well, we were sent out here to do a job, and we're doing it, and we'll stay here until it's done.
> Journalist: Thank you.

10. In March 1966, President Johnson, talking about Vietnam with Columbia University historian Henry Graff, said "proudly" (as Graff reported it): "I wanted to leave the footprints of America there."

Isolated oddities can, on investigation, prove to be deviations from an otherwise healthy set of circumstances. Or they may turn out to be small symptoms of a more generalized malady. In such a case, investigation may disclose larger absurdities:

1. The most powerful nation in the world, producing 60 percent of the world's wealth, using the most advanced weapons known to military science short of atomic bombs, has been unable to defeat an army of peasants, at first armed with homemade and captured weapons, then with modern firearms supplied from outside, but still without an air force, navy, or heavy artillery.

2. Declaring its intent to preserve freedom, the United States has supported a succession of military dictatorships in South Vietnam.

3. Again and again President Johnson has insisted that American forces are in Vietnam to repel "aggression" and that "if they'll go home tomorrow, we'll go home." Our actions in South Vietnam have been conducted against a force of which 80 percent to 90 percent are already home (that is, in South Vietnam, where they are from) with the rest from North Vietnam, which is not very far from home. Indeed, if the Geneva Accords are to be taken as a basis (as the United States itself agrees), it is all one country, and all our opponents are home. The main fighting against these Vietnamese is conducted now by 350,000 Americans, all of whom are quite far from home, plus 40,000 Koreans, who also are definitely not home. In bombing North Vietnam, our fliers who are not home, are killing people who are.

4. Government officials have declared that we are at war in Vietnam to stop Chinese "expansion." Available evidence is that there are no Chinese troops in Vietnam, nor anywhere else outside of China. China is, indeed, half encircled by American military bases in Korea, Japan, the Philippines, Formosa, Okinawa, and Thailand—with about 250,000 United States soldiers, sailors, and airmen at those bases.

5. The United States maintains it must continue fighting in Vietnam so as not to lose prestige among its allies. As the war has continued, the prestige of the United States in Japan (its most important ally in Asia) and in England, France, and West Germany (its most important allies in Europe) has seriously declined.

"Absurdity" is in the mind of the viewer; it involves a simple mental operation. We come across what in itself seems an ordinary fact, but when we place it alongside another fact, we find an incongruity. That other fact may come out of the common pile which most people share or it may come out of the viewer's own life experience. Thus to see a situation as absurd does not depend on the number of facts we know about a situation, but on the way we relate the facts we know—on what we pull out of our memories when a fact presents itself.

Likewise, making moral judgments—as on the war in Vietnam—does not depend mainly on the volume of our knowledge. We find, indeed, that the experts in each field disagree sharply on the most fundamental questions. This is because ethical decisions depend on the relationships in which we place the facts we know.

Therefore what we bring to the common body of evidence in Vietnam—the *perspective* we have—is crucial. It determines what we choose to see or not to see. It determines how we relate the things we see. This perspective varies from one person to another. I think we get closer to wisdom, and also to democracy, when we add the perspectives of other people to our own.

What I want to do in this book is to focus my vision, coming from my own set of experiences, on the data of public record: government documents, newspaper reports, the published work of scholars. To begin, then, I should say a little about the biases that affect my view of the war in Vietnam.

In the midst of World War II, I enlisted in the United States Air Force and flew as a bombardier in the European theater of operations. From beginning to end, I believed fervently that Hitler's force had to be met with force. But when I was packing and labeling my folder of war days and mementos to go home, I impulsively marked it "Never Again."

I had participated in at least one atrocity, and I came away from the war with several conclusions:

(1) that innocent and well-meaning people—of whom I considered myself one—are capable of the most brutal acts and the most self-righteous excuses, whether they be Germans, Japanese, Russians, or Americans;

(2) that one of the guiding rules for an Air Force in possession of large quantities of bombs is: "Get rid of them—anywhere";

(3) that the claims of statesmen and military men to be bombing only "military targets" should not be taken seriously;

(4) that war is a monstrously wasteful way of achieving a social objective, always involving indiscriminate mass slaughter unconnected with that objective; that even World War II, with its stark moral issues—the "best" of all wars—presented agonizing moral questions; and that any situation where right and wrong were *not* so clear, and where human life was being sacrificed, should be regarded with deep suspicion.

Later I was trained as a historian and learned that our country is capable of moral absurdities. There was the Spanish-American War, described by an American diplomat as a "splendid little war," though it reeked of corpses on Cuban hillsides and rotten meat fed to soldiers—thousands of whom died of food poisoning.

There were our warships cannonading Vera Cruz in 1914, with hundreds of Mexican civilians killed, because the Mexicans refused to give a twenty-one-gun salute to the American flag.

There was Haiti in 1915, where United States Marines brought "order" by shooting 2,000 Haitians, with an Admiral wiring the Secretary of the Navy: "Next Thursday...I will permit Congress to elect a President."

There was President McKinley's decision to "civilize" the Filipinos, and Andrew Carnegie's subsequent message to a friend who defended our crushing of the Filipino rebellion: "It is a matter of congratulaton that you seem to have about finished your work of civilizing the Filipinos. It is thought that about 8,000 of them have been completely civilized and sent to Heaven."

My conclusion was not that the United States was more evil than other nations, only that she was just as evil (although she sometimes had more finesse). It does not take too much study of modern history to conclude that nations as a lot tend to be vicious.

My work in American history led to another idea: that there is no necessary relationship between liberalism in domestic policy and humaneness in foreign policy. Some of our most grotesquely immoral deeds have been committed by "liberals." Take Andrew Jackson's murderous attitude toward the Indians (whom we treated, ironically, as a foreign nation) in the bloody Trail of Tears, or Progressive Theodore Roosevelt's bullying activities in the Caribbean. Take Woodrow Wilson's behavior towards Haiti and Mexico and his carrying the nation, for reasons still inexplicable, into the pointless savagery of the First World War.

During a year off from teaching, I did research on modern Chinese history as a Fellow at the Harvard Center for East Asian Studies. I soon became aware of a great gap between the findings of scholars and the policy of the United States. Official policy seemed to be derived more from lurid headlines in the press than from the balanced findings of the academicians. It was not that the reports of "thought control" in China were wrong; it was that so much else that China had accomplished was ignored. It was not that the Chinese were not aggressive in their statements about the United States; it was that their foreign policy was quite restrained for a proud nation with a new regime. It was not that there was not much that was wrong in Communist China; it was that American policy-makers acted as if there was not much that was wrong with the United States.

This last point was important; the moral failures of other nations had to be seen not in isolation, but against our own failures. It was in this connection that another part of my life influenced my perspective on the problem of Vietnam: my years of living and teaching in a Negro community in the deep South and my involvement in some of the civil rights struggles of the early 1960s. That experience has given me a glimpse of American foreign policy from a special standpoint, one which I will try to explain in the third chapter of this book.

There is one final influence on my thinking which I should mention: the perspective of geographical distance, beginning to see American policy as people in a far-off country saw it. There are many Americans in recent years—Peace Corpsmen, travelers, students—who have been startled by a sudden awareness of how other people see us. My own recent experience was with Japan, and I want to discuss this in the next chapter.

On the basis of these angles of vision, brought to bear on the historical record of the Vietnam war, I am going to argue in the following pages that the United States should withdraw its military forces from Vietnam.

Thus far almost all of the nationally known critics of our Vietnam policy—perceptive as they are—have been reluctant to call for the withdrawal of the United States from Vietnam. Sometimes this is for substantive reasons, which I will discuss later on. But often, I believe, it is because these critics consider total military withdrawal, while logical and right, "too extreme" as a tactical position, and therefore unpalatable to the public and unlikely to be adopted as national policy.

Scholars, who pride themselves on speaking their minds, often engage in a form of self-censorship which is called "realism." To be "realistic" in dealing with a problem is to work only among the alternatives which the most powerful in society put forth. It is as if we are all confined to a, b, c, or d in the multiple choice test, when we know there is another possible answer. American society, although it has more freedom of expression than most societies in the world, thus sets limits beyond which respectable people are not supposed to think or speak. So far, too much of the debate on Vietnam has observed these limits.

To me this is a surrender of the role of the citizen in a democracy. The citizen's job, I believe, is to declare firmly what he thinks is right. To compromise with politicians from the very start is to end with a compromise of a compromise. This weakens the moral force of a citizenry which has little enough strength in the shaping of governmental policy. Machiavelli cautioned the prince not to adopt the ethics of the citizen. It is appropriate now to suggest to the Citizen that he cannot, without sacrificing both integrity and power, adopt the ethics of the Prince.

15

What Did
Richard Nixon Learn?

No one American president can be blamed wholly for the disastrous U.S. military assault on Vietnam. The long line of blame, if we really stretch, can go as far back as Franklin D. Roosevelt, who spoke to the world of self determination but gave the French secret assurances that they would not be expelled from their colony in Indochina, comprising Vietnam, Laos, and Cambodia. Presidents Harry Truman and Dwight Eisenhower gave massive military aid to the French in their war against the Vietnamese independence movement. John F. Kennedy began the military escalation by sending the first large contingents of American troops and using U.S. warplanes to bomb Vietnam. Lyndon Johnson then carried on the major escalation of the war, with all-out bombing, and 525,000 troops. Nixon extended the war to Laos and Cambodia, but finally saw the need to sign a peace treaty which called for U.S. withdrawal. Ten years after the end of the war he wrote about his role in a memoir: *No More Vietnams*. I reviewed his book, as follows, in the Madison, Wisconsin *Capital Times* in May of 1985.

Richard Nixon has learned nothing from the Vietnam experience. And now he wants to teach us what he has learned. Let's examine his strange analysis.

Trying to persuade a public made skeptical by decades of lies, Nixon repeats a much-used formula to justify our war in Vietnam: "Events since 1975 have proved..."

The argument goes like this: Vietnam is now a dictatorial country, run by communists, from which a million people have fled due to political repression and economic disorder. That proves we were right to turn that country into a wasteland, to denude its forests, ruin its crop land, and kill over a million people, by raining millions of tons of bombs, napalm, Agent Orange, and various terror devices on peasant men, women and children.

Let's see where such logic takes us. Suppose the United States had "won," which, as Nixon tells us, would have required even more violence (killing another million people, destroying another thousand villages, leaving another thousand children without arms and legs, killing another 10,000 and 20,000 GIs and adding to the number of Americans who now wear artificial limbs?).

How would that have ensured a democratic and economically sound, independent Vietnam, when the government in Saigon that we supported was itself a brutal dictatorship, totally dependent on the U.S. military, abhorred by most Vietnamese? In Korea we "saved" South Korea, and we ended up as we had started, with a dictatorship in North Korea, a dictatorship in South Korea, but with one difference: two million people were dead.

Perhaps we should look at other situations where the U.S., intervening in another country to "stop communism," did indeed "win."

Take Guatemala, where the CIA in 1954 successfully overthrew a left-leaning government that had dared to take back the huge estates of the United Fruit Corporation. What was the result? One of the most ugly military dictatorships in the world has ruled Guatemala since that "victory"—death squads, mass executions of peasants, miserable conditions for the Indians who are a majority of that country.

Or, take another case where we "won"—Chile, where, with the help of the CIA and IT&T, the Marxist Allende was overthrown. (Both Allende in Chile and Arbenz in Guatemala became president through remarkably democratic elections.) The result of that "victory" was the horror of General Pinochet, of which we get a glimpse in the film *Missing*—the disappearance of thousands of people, the streets patrolled by soldiers with machine guns, the atmosphere and reality of fascism.

There is not much to choose between the results of military interventions whether by the United States or the Soviet Union. The logic of military interventions is that they produce tyrannies, but that is considered a "victory" if the tyranny is friendly to the intervening power.

If the Soviets are forced to beat a retreat from Afghanistan, perhaps some Soviet Nixon will write a book explaining why they should have used more force, and how things would have been much better if they had won.

Nixon's "history" of the Vietnam War is a desperate attempt to make a silk purse out of a sow's behind. There is room to note only a few of his falsehoods and omissions.

War is war, he says, so why get excited over a million or two million deaths? Especially since it was "a cause that was worth fighting for."

Ask the veterans of Vietnam. Ask the families of the dead. Ask the amputees and walking wounded. Yes, some will insist it was a good cause; who wants to think lives were lost for nothing? But most are bitter and angry.

Hundreds of thousands of GIs gave their commentary on that "cause" by walking away from the war: desertions, AWOLs, mutinous behavior, leading to 250,000 undesirable, bad conduct, or dishonorable discharges, and 300,000 more less-than-honorable discharges.

There was a powerful anti-war movement among GIs, even extending to pilots who refused to fly those last vicious raids on the residential areas and hospitals of Hanoi and Haiphong.

Read *Bloods* by *Time* reporter Wallace Terry, with its oral histories of black GIs, who died at twice the rate of whites. See if they thought it "a cause worth fighting for." Consider also the 570,000 draft refusers, of whom very few were peace activists. Most of them were poor white and black kids who just didn't register or didn't show up for induction, so little heart did they have for a heartless war.

"Excessive casualties" among civilians? Oh, no! Nixon says. That is "bizarre," he says, because our forces "operated under strict rules of engagement," Nixon is bizarre (I speak as an ex-Air Force bombardier). Can jet planes, flying a high altitudes, dropping seven million tons of bombs (three times the total tonnage dropped in WW II), possibly operate under "strict rules of engagement"?

Hasn't Nixon read the Pentagon Papers, the official top secret Defense Department history of the Vietnam War, where it is clear that bombing was undertaken to destroy the morale of the population? Was the massacre of terrified women holding babies in their arms in the village of My Lai an "isolated incident"?

Col. Oran Henderson, charged with covering up My Lai, told reporters: "Every unit of brigade size has its My Lai hidden someplace."

Surely Nixon has read the book that fearlessly tries to justify U.S. policy in Vietnam, Guenter Lewy's *America in Vietnam*, where Lewy himself admits that the Vietnamese were "subjected to random bombardment by artillery and aircraft" and "indiscriminate killings" in the populated Delta area which "took a heavy toll of essentially men, women and children."

We tried to save South Vietnam from invasion by the North, Nixon repeats. The evidence against this, from the government's own records, is mountainous.

"South Vietnam was essentially the creation of the United States," the Pentagon historians wrote, not knowing their words would be released to the public. How can it possibly be argued that the U.S. cared about self determination for the Vietnamese when it did everything it could (and even proposed atomic bombing) to have the French retain control of their colony?

Nixon falsifies the record:

Despite his public statements, President Franklin Roosevelt privately assured the French they could retain control of Vietnam; the documentation is in the Pentagon Papers.

Invasion from the North? Most of the southern countryside was in rebellion against Diem, whom the United States had installed in power, flying him in from New Jersey! These southern rebels in the National Liberation Front had developed what Douglas Pike (a U.S. government analyst) admitted was the most popular mass organization in the history of the country. And the Pentagon historians wrote:

"Only the Viet Cong had any real support and influence on a broad base in the countryside."

Did we intervene only after there was invasion from the North? The first battalion of 500 North Vietnamese, according to U.S. Intelligence data, did not arrive until late 1964 or early 1965. By then there were 40,000 U.S. troops and thousands of bombing sorties had been flown by American pilots, as early as 1962 and 1963.

There was one foreign invader in Vietnam—the U.S. Army.

Congress—with its traditional cowardice, and based on lies told by President Lyndon Johnson, Secretary of State Dean Rusk, and Secretary of Defense Robert McNamara about the supposed attacks on American vessels in the Gulf of Tonkin in 1964—had given LBJ a blank check for mass murder.

It was not Congress that stopped the war, though Nixon blames them. It was the American people, who by 1969 overwhelmingly rejected the war and wanted out.

Why is Nixon writing all this nonsense now? What he seems to want is to persuade us that we didn't kill enough GIs and Vietnamese in Vietnam. If we had killed more, we might have "won." Therefore, we must not be so hesitant in Central America.

But before we rush to send the boys and drop the bombs in Central America, or even just to supply our unsavory allies there, so Latins can kill Latins while the Dow Jones average goes up, we might reconsider the "cause that was worth fighting for." That cause has something to do with stopping Communism.

Before we get intoxicated, as Nixon and Reagan seem to be, on this anti-communist whiskey that has led to so much drunken driving in the world, such huge death tolls, we ought to stop and think.

It is useful to have Nixon back. He reminds us that he and Reagan are one—the discredited ex-president and the credited new president—brandishing a shining credit card for war that he wants to flash all over the world.

But the bill will be sent to us, not just in dollars, but in human lives. These blokes mean no good for the people of the United States, not for this generation, not for our children or our grandchildren.

16

Whom Will We Honor on Memorial Day?

In 1974, I was invited by Tom Winship, the editor of the *Boston Globe*, who had been bold enough in 1971 to print part of the top-secret Pentagon Papers on the history of the Vietnam War, to write a bi-weekly column for the op-ed page of the newspaper. I did that for about a year and a half. The column below appeared June 2, 1976, in connection with that year's Memorial Day. After it appeared, my column was cancelled.

M emorial Day will be celebrated as usual, by high-speed collisions of automobiles and bodies strewn on highways and the sound of ambulance sirens throughout the land.

It will also be celebrated by the display of flags, the sound of bugles and drums, by parades and speeches and unthinking applause.

It will be celebrated by giant corporations, which make guns, bombs, fighter planes, aircraft carriers and an endless assortment of military junk and which await the $100 billion in contracts to be approved soon by Congress and the President.

Memorial Day will be celebrated in other words, by the usual betray-

al of the dead, by the hypocritical patriotism of the politicians and con-
tractors preparing for more wars, more graves to receive more flowers on
future Memorial Days.

The memory of the dead deserves a different dedication. To peace, to
defiance of governments.

There was a young woman in New Hampshire who refused to allow
her husband, killed in Vietnam, to be given a military burial. She rejected
the hollow ceremony ordered by those who sent him and 50,000 others
to their deaths. Her courage should be cherished on Memorial Day.

There were the B52 pilots who refused to fly those last vicious raids
of Nixon's and Kissinger's war. Have any of the great universities, so quick
to give honorary degrees to God-knows-whom, thought to honor those
men at this Commencement time, on this Memorial Day?

No politician who voted funds for war, no business contractor for the
military, no general who ordered young men into battle, no FBI man
who spied on anti-war activities, should be invited to public ceremonies
on this sacred day. Let the dead of past wars he honored. Let those who
live pledge themselves never to embark on mass slaughter again.

"The shell had his number on it. The blood ran into the ground....
Where his chest ought to have been they pinned the Congressional
Medal, the DSC, the Medaille Militaire, the Belgian Croix de Guerre, the
Italian gold medal, The Vitutea Militara sent by Queen Marie of
Rumania. All the Washingtonians brought flowers. Woodrow Wilson
brought a bouquet of poppies."

Those are the concluding lines of John Dos Passos' angry novel *1919*.
Let us honor him on Memorial Day.

And also Thoreau, who went to jail to protest the Mexican War.

And Mark Twain, who denounced our war against the Filipinos at
the turn of the century.

And I.F. Stone, who virtually alone among newspaper editors
exposed the fraud and brutality of the Korean War.

Let us honor Martin Luther King, who refused the enticements of
the White House, and the cautions of associates, and thundered against
the war in Vietnam.

Memorial Day should be a day for putting flowers on graves and planting trees. Also, for destroying the weapons of death that endanger us more than they protect us, that waste our resources and threaten our children and grandchildren.

On Memorial Day we should take note that, in the name of "defense," our taxes have been used to spend a quarter of a billion dollars on a helicopter assault ship called "the biggest floating lemon," which was accepted by the Navy although it had over 2,000 major defects at the time of its trial cruise.

Meanwhile, there is such a shortage of housing that millions live in dilapidated sections of our cities and millions more are forced to pay high rents or high interest rates on their mortgages.

There's 90 billion for the B1 bomber, but people don't have money to pay hospital bills.

We must be practical, say those whose practicality has consisted of a war every generation. We mustn't deplete our defenses. Say those who have depleted our youth, stolen our resources.

In the end, it is living people, not corpses, creative energy, not destructive rage, which are our only real defense, not just against other governments trying to kill us, but against our own, also trying to kill us.

Let us not set out, this Memorial Day, on the same old drunken ride to death.

PART 6

On
World War II

17

Saving Private Ryan

Hollywood has always loved war. Not only are war movies popular and profitable, but they create a partnership between the
movie industry and the government, thus violating the principle of independence in art. Indeed, at times, the government
will subsidize such movies, lending its equipment for war
scenes, giving its material support and official approval for a
war-mongering movie of the Vietnam era, *The Green Berets*.
Saving Private Ryan, the movie, recalled to me the glorification
of World War II which has persisted in our culture for over fifty
years, and fitted perfectly the martial spirit of Hollywood. I
thought it needed a critical eye.

Like so many World War II veterans (I could see them all around me
in the theater audience) I was drawn to see *Saving Private Ryan*. I had
volunteered for the Air Force at the age of 20, and after training as a
bombardier went overseas with my crew to fly, out of England, the last
bombing missions of the European war.

My pilot was 19, my tail gunner was 18. Every death in *Saving
Private Ryan* reminded me, as other veterans were reminded, of how
lucky we were, we who survived. My two closest Air Force buddies, who

went through training with me and then to other theaters (what a word for that, "theaters"!)—Joe Perry to Italy, Ed Plotkin to the Pacific—were killed in the last weeks of the war.

I watched the extraordinarily photographed battle scenes, thoroughly taken in. But when the movie was over I realized that it was exactly that—I had been taken in—and I disliked the film intensely, indeed, was angry at it. Because I did not want the suffering of men in war to be used, yes, exploited, in such a way as to revive what should be buried along with all those bodies in Arlington Cemetery—the glory of military heroism.

"The greatest war movie ever made," the film critics say, about *Saving Private Ryan*. They are a disappointing lot, the film critics. They are excited, even exultant, about the brilliant cinematography, depicting the bloody chaos of the Omaha Beach landing. But they are pitifully superficial.

They fail (with a few honorable exceptions, like Vincent Canby in *The New York Times*, Donald Murray in the *Boston Globe*) to ask the most important question: will this film help persuade the next generation that such scenes must never occur again? Will it make clear that war must be resisted, even if accompanied by the seductive speeches of political leaders saying that this latest war, unlike other bad wars we remember, will be another "good" one, like World War II?

The admiring critics of the movie give the answer to that by their own words: it is a war movie. Not an anti-war movie. Some viewers have said: how can anyone want to go to war after seeing such horror? But knowing the horrors of war has never been an obstacle to a quick build-up of war spirit by patriotic political speeches and an obsequious press.

All that bloodshed, all that pain, all those torn limbs and exposed intestines will not deter a brave people from going to war. They just need to believe that the cause is just. They need to be told: it is a war to end all wars (Woodrow Wilson) or we need to stop Communism (Kennedy, Johnson, Nixon), or aggression must not go unpunished (Bush).

In *Saving Private Ryan* there is never any doubt that the cause is just. This is the good war. There is no need to say the words explicitly. The crosses stand heartrendingly mute in Arlington National Cemetery. A benign General Marshall, front and back of the movie, quotes Abraham Lincoln's words of solace to a mother who has lost five sons, leaving no doubt that this war, like that one, while it causes sorrow to a million mothers, is in a good cause.

Yes, getting rid of fascism was a good cause. But does that unquestionably make it a good war? The war corrupted us, did it not. The hate it engendered was not confined to Nazis. We put Japanese families in concentration camps. We killed huge numbers of innocent people—the word "atrocity" fits—in our bombings of Dresden, Hamburg, Tokyo, and finally Hiroshima and Nagasaki. And when the war ended we and our Allies began preparing for another, this time with nuclear weapons, which if used would make Hitler's Holocaust look puny.

We can argue endlessly over whether there was an alternative in the short run, whether fascism could have been resisted without 50 million dead. But the long-term effect of World War II on the thinking of the world was pernicious and deep. It made war, so thoroughly discredited by the senseless slaughter of World War I, noble once again. It enabled political leaders, whatever miserable adventure they would take us into, whatever mayhem they would wreak on other people (2 million dead in Korea, at least that many in Southeast Asia, hundreds of thousands in Iraq) and on our own, to invoke World War II as a model.

Communism supplanted Nazism as a reason for war, and when Communism could no longer be pointed to as a threat, a convenient enemy, like Saddam Hussein, could be compared to Hitler. Glib analogies were used to justify immense suffering. The presumed absolute goodness of World War II created an aura of rightness around war itself (note the absence of a great movement of protest against the Korean War) which only an adventure as monstrously evil, as soaked in official lies as Vietnam, could dispel.

Vietnam caused large numbers of Americans to question the enterprise of war itself. Now *Saving Private Ryan*, aided by superb cinematographic technology, draws on our deep feeling for the GIs in order to rescue, not just Private Ryan, but the good name of war. I will not be surprised if Spielberg gets an Academy Award. Did not Kissinger get a Nobel Prize? The committees that give prizes are, too often, innocent of social conscience. But we are not bound to honor their choices.

To refresh my memory of it, I watched the video of *All Quiet on the Western Front*. With no musical background, without the benefit of modern cinematography, without fields of corpses, with no pools of blood reddening the screen, the horror of trench warfare as experienced by infantrymen was conveyed more powerfully than in *Saving Private Ryan*. The one fleeting shot of two hands clutching barbed wire, the rest of the body gone, said it all.

In Spielberg's film we see Tom Hanks gunned down, and it is sad. But it is a prosaic sadness compared to the death of the protagonist in Erich Remarque's story, as we watch a butterfly hover over a trench and we see the hand of Lew Ayres reach out for it, and go limp. We see no dead body, only that beautiful butterfly, and the reaching hand.

But more important, *All Quiet on the Western Front* does not dodge, as *Saving Private Ryan* does, as its gushing critics do, the issue of war. In it, war is not just horrible, it is futile. It is not inevitable, it is manufactured. Back home, commenting on the war, is no kindly General Marshall, quoting Lincoln, but prosperous men urging the soldiers, "On to Paris, boys! On to Paris!"

The boys in the trenches don't just discuss the battle, they discuss the war: Who is profiting? Hey, let's have the world's leaders get into an arena and fight it out themselves! We have no quarrel with the boys on the other side of the barbed wire!

Our culture is in deep trouble when a film like *Saving Private Ryan* can pass by, like a military parade, with nothing but a shower of confetti and hurrahs for its color and grandeur. But surely, it is nothing new that people with moral sensibility must create their own culture.

18

The Bombing
of Royan

In mid-April of 1945, a combined air-ground attack com-
pleted the destruction of the French seaside resort of Royan,
a town of ancient chateaux and lovely beaches (a favorite
spot of Picasso), on the Atlantic coast near Bordeaux. It was
ten months after D-day, the invasion of Western Europe by
Allied Forces—and three weeks before the final surrender
of Germany. The official history of the U.S. Army Air Forces
in World War II refers briefly to the attack on Royan:

> On the 14 through 16 April more than 1,200 American heavies
> went out each day to drop incendiaries, napalm bombs, and
> 2,000-pound demolition bombs on stubborn German garrisons
> still holding out around Bordeaux. The bombing was effective,
> and French forces soon occupied the region.

According to the official history those bombs were
dropped "on stubborn German garrisons." This is mislead-
ing. The bombs were dropped in the general vicinity of
Royan, where there were German garrisons (mostly outside the town) and where there were also civilian occu-

pants of the town. It was my participation in this mission, as a bombardier with the 490th Bomb Group, that prompted me, after the war, to inquire into the bombing of Royan. At the time, it seemed just another bombing mission, with a slightly different target, and a slightly different cargo of bombs. We were awakened in the early hours of morning, went to the briefing, where we were told our job was to bomb pockets of German troops remaining in and around Royan, and that in our bomb bays were thirty 100-pound bombs containing "jellied gasoline," a new substance (now known as napalm). Our bombs were not precisely directed at German installations but were dropped by toggle switch over the Royan area, on seeing the bombs of the lead ship leave the bomb bay—a device good for saturation bombing, not pinpoint bombing (aside from the fact that the Norden bombsight, which we were trained to use, could not be counted on to hit enemy installations and miss nearby civilians from a height of 25,000 feet). The toggle switch was connected to an intervalometer which automatically dropped the bombs, after the first fell, in a timed sequence. I remember distinctly seeing, from our great height, the bombs explode in the town, flaring like matches struck in fog. I was completely unaware of the human chaos below.

In 1966, I spent some time in Royan and found in the town library most of the material on which this essay is based.

A letter from Colonel H. A. Schmidt, of the Office of the Chief of Military History, Department of the Army, responding to my request for information on the bombing of Royan, stated:

The liberation of the port of Bordeaux required the reduction of the bridgeheads of Royan, la Pointe, de Grave and Oléron. The Royan sector was the principal German garrison holding out in the Bordeaux area, and first priority in the operations. The Eighth U.S. Air Force paved the way of the Allied ground forces by massive bombing.

The quick, casual description of potentially embarrassing episodes is common in histories written by men in government. Winston Churchill, who was Prime Minister when the city of Dresden was indiscriminately saturated with fire-bombs in February 1945, leaving 135,000 dead, and who had approved the general strategy of bombing urban areas, confined himself to this comment in his memoirs: "We made a heavy raid in the latter month on Dresden, then a centre of communications of Germany's Eastern front."[*]

Strenuous arguments were made for the bombing attacks on Hiroshima and Dresden on the basis of military necessity, although ultimately the evidence was overwhelmingly against such arguments. In the case of Royan, it was virtually impossible to even launch a defense of the attack on grounds of military need. It was a small town on the Atlantic coast, far from the fighting front. True, it commanded the sea entrance to Bordeaux, a great port. But this was not crucially needed. Without Bordeaux, and later without its port facilities, the Allies had invaded Normandy, taken Paris, crossed the Rhine, and were now well into Germany. Furthermore, the general air-ground assault on Royan took place three weeks before the end of the war in Europe, at a time when everyone knew it would all soon be over and all one had to do for the surrender of the German garrisons in the area was to wait.[**]

---

[*] David Irving, *The Destruction of Dresden*, Part II, esp. Ch. II, "Thunderclap," which shows the part Churchill played in pushing the massive raids on cities in Eastern Germany; and Part V, Ch. II, where Churchill later seems to be trying to put the blame on the Bomber Command.

[**] Also, in a remark I must confine to a footnote as a gesture to the equality of all victims: there was something to distinguish Royan from both Hiroshima and Dresden; its population was, at least officially, friend, not foe.

Nevertheless, on April 14, 1945, the attack on Royan began, reported as follows in a dispatch from London the next day to *The New York Times:*

> The full weight of the United States Eighth Air Force was hurled yesterday against one of Europe's forgotten fronts, the German-held pocket in the Gironde Estuary commanding the great southwestern French port of Bordeaux. The blow by 1,150 Flying Fortresses and Liberators, without fighter escort, preceded a limited land attack by French troops....
>
> Some 30,000 to 40,000 Nazi troops have been holed up in the Gironde Estuary pocket since the tides of war swept around and past them last summer.... The striking force was probably the biggest heavy bombing fleet ever sent out from Britain in daylight without escorting fighters. Five of the big planes failed to return.

Was the air raid worth even the loss of only five air crews—forty-five men? That was just the tip of the tragedy, counted in lives lost, homes destroyed, persons wounded and burned. For the next day, April 15, the attack was heavier, and the airplanes had a new weapon. A front-page dispatch in *The New York Times* from Paris reported "two days of shattering aerial bombardment and savage ground attacks in the drive to open the port of Bordeaux." It went on:

> More than 1,300 Flying Fortresses and Liberators of the United States Eighth Air Force prepared the way for today's successful assault by drenching the enemy's positions on both sides of the Gironde controlling the route to Bordeaux with about 460,000 gallons of liquid fire that bathed in flames the German positions and strong points....
>
> It was the first time that the Eighth Air Force had employed its new bomb. The inflammable substance is dropped in tanks that are exploded on impact by detonators that ignite the fuel, splashing the flaming contents of each tank over an area of approximately sixty square yards.

The liquid fire was napalm, used for the first time in warfare. The following day, there was another bombing, with high explosive bombs, and further ground assaults. Altogether, it took three days of bombing and land attacks to bring the Germans in the area to surrender. The French ground forces suffered about two hundred dead; the Germans lost several hundred. There is no accurate count on the civilian dead resulting from those attacks, but *The New York Times* dispatch by a correspondent in the area reported:

> French troops mopped up most of Royan, on the north side of the river's mouth.... Royan, a town of 20,000, once was a vacation spot. About 350 civilians, dazed or bruised by two terrific air bombings in forty-eight hours, crawled from the ruins and said the air attacks had been "such hell as we never believed possible."

In a few weeks, the war was over in Europe. The town of Royan, "liberated," was totally in ruins.

That eve-of-victory attack in mid-April 1945 was the second disaster suffered by Royan at the hands of the Allied forces. On January 5, 1945, in the darkness before dawn, two waves of heavy British bombers, about an hour apart, flew over Royan, which was still inhabited, despite a voluntary evacuation in the preceding months, by about two thousand persons. There was no warning, there were no shelters. The bombs were dropped in the heart of the city (completely missing the German troops, who were outside) within a rectangle marked out by flares dropped by one of the planes. Over a thousand people were killed (some of the estimates are twelve hundred, others fourteen hundred). Several hundred people were wounded. Almost every building in Royan was demolished. The later attack in April, came therefore, on the ruins of buildings and the remnants of families, and made the annihilation of the city complete.

That January bombing has never been adequately explained. One phrase recurs in all the accounts—"*une tragique erreur.*" The explanation given by military officials at the time was that the bombers were originally scheduled to bomb in Germany, but because of bad weather there, were rerouted to Royan without a map of the German positions. French planes from nearby Cognac were supposed to mark the positions with flares but this was either not done, or done badly, or the flares were carried away by the wind.*

A dispatch written by a local person soon after that bombing, entitled "La Nuit Tragique," contained this description:**

> Under the German occupation. It is night, calm reigns over the sleeping town, Midnight sounds in the Royan church. Then one o'clock, then two.... The Royannais sleep, muffled against the chill. Three, four o'clock. A humming is heard in the distance. Rockets light up the sky. The inhabitants are not afraid; they are tranquil, because they know that Allied airplanes, if these are such, will aim at the German fortifications, and besides, is this not the evening when German supply planes come in? The clock sounds five. Then follows the catastrophe, brutal, horrible, implacable. A deluge of steel and fire descended on Royan; a wave of 350 planes lets go 800 tons of bombs on the town. Some seconds later, the survivors are calling for aid to the wounded. Cries, death rattles.... A woman appeals for help, her head appears alone, her body crushed under an enormous beam.
>
> ...A whole family is imprisoned in a cave, the water mounts. The rescuers lift their heads—this humming, yet, it is another wave of planes. This achieves the complete destruction of Royan and its inhabitants. Royan has gone down with the civilized world, by the error, the bestiality, the folly of man. (Royan a sombré en même temps que le monde civillisé, par l'erreur, la bêtise et la folie des hommes.)

Eight days after the attack, an article appeared in *La Libération* appealing for help: "American friends, you whose Florida beaches have never known such hours, take charge of the reconstruction of Royan!"

---

* This is repeated as late as 1965 in Dr. J.R. Colle's book, *Royan, son passé, ses environs* (La Rochelle, 1965), who summarizes the incident in his chapter, "La Résistance et La Libération."

** The periodical in which the article appeared is no longer available, but the article, along with many others to which I will refer, was collected in a remarkable little book, produced by a printer in Royan, a former member of the Resistance (Botton, Père et fils) in 1965, entitled: *Royan—Ville Martyre*. The translations are mine. A bitter introductory note by Ulysse Botton speaks of "*la tuerie*" (the slaughter) of January 5, 1945. There is a picture of the rebuilt Royan, modern buildings instead of ancient châteaux. "Our visitors, French and foreign vacationers, should thus learn, if they do not know it, that this new town and this modern architecture proceed from a murder, to this day neither admitted nor penalized..."

In 1948, General de Larminat, who was in charge of French forces in the West (that is, the Bordeaux region) for the last six months of the war, broke a long silence to reply to bitter criticism of both the January and April bombings by local leaders. He exonerated the French military command at Cognac, saying they were not responsible for directing the English planes to Royan. It was, rather, a "tragic error" by the Allied Command; the whole episode was one of the unfortunate consequences of war:[*]

> Will we draw from this an excuse to attack our Allies, who gave countless lives to liberate our country? That would be profoundly unjust. All wars carry these painful errors. Where is the infantryman of 1914-18, and of this war, who has not received friendly shells, badly aimed? How many French towns, how many combat units, have suffered bombings by mistake at the hands of allied planes? This is the painful ransom, the inevitable ransom of war, against which it is vain to protest, about which it is vain to quarrel. We pay homage to those who died in the war, we help the survivors and repair the ruins; but we do not linger on the causes of these unfortunate events because, in truth there is only a single cause: War, and the only ones truly responsible are those who wanted war.

(Compare this with the explanation of the Dresden bombing given by Air Marshal Sir Robert Saundby:

> It was one of those terrible things that sometimes happen in wartime, brought about by an unfortunate combination of circumstances. Those who approved it were neither wicked nor cruel, though it may well be that they were too remote from the harsh realities of war to understand fully the appalling destructive power of air bombardment in the spring of 1945....
> It is not so much this or the other means of making war that is immoral or inhumane. What is immoral is war itself. Once full-scale war

---

*Botton collection. This is of course, a widely held view: "c'est la guerre" —a resigned, unhappy surrender to inevitability. We find it again in *Le Pays d'Ouest*, a postwar periodical, now defunct, which published an article, "Le Siège et Attaque de Royan," saying: "Whatever the reason, the bombardment of Royan on January 5, 1945, must be considered among the regrettable errors that unfortunately it is hard to avoid in the course of the extremely complicated operations of modern war."

has broken out it can never be humanized or civilized, and if one side attempted to do so it would be most likely to be defeated. So long as we resort to war to settle differences between nations, so long will we have to endure the horrors, the barbarities and excesses that war brings with it. That, to me, is the lesson of Dresden.)

Some important evidence on the January bombing appeared in 1966 with the publication of the memoirs of Admiral Hubert Meyer, French commander in the Rochefort-La Rochelle area (the two Atlantic ports just north of Royan). Meyer, in September and October 1944, when the Germans, having fled west from the Allied invasion in northern France, were consolidating their pockets on the Atlantic coast, had begun negotiation with the German commander of La Rochelle-Rochefort, Admiral Schirlitz. In effect, they agreed that the Germans would not blow up the port installations, and in return the French would not attack the Germans. Then the Germans evacuated Rochefort, moving north into the La Rochelle area, to lines both sides agreed on.

In late December 1944, Meyer was asked to travel south along the coast from Rochefort to Royan, where the second German coastal pocket was under the command of Admiral Michahelles, to negotiate a prisoner exchange. In the course of these talks, he was told that the German admiral was disposed to sign an agreement to hold the military *status quo* around Royan, as had been done by Schirlitz at Rochefort-La Rochelle. Meyer pointed out that Royan was different, that the Allies might have to attack the Germans there because Royan commanded Bordeaux, where free passage of goods was needed to supply the Southwest. The Germans, to Meyer's surprise, replied that they might agree to open Bordeaux to all but military supplies.

Conveying this offer to the French military headquarters at Saintes and Cognac, Meyer received a cool response. The French generals could not give a sound military reason for insisting on an attack, but pointed to "*l'aspect moral.*" It would be hard, said General d'Anselme, "to frustrate an ardent desire for battle—a battle where victory was certain—by the army of the Southwest, which had been champing at the bit for months."*

Meyer said the morale of the troops was not worth the sacrifice of a town and hundreds of lives for a limited objective, when the war was virtually won, that they did not have the right to kill a single man when the adversary had offered a truce.**

Further discussion, he was told, would have to await the return of General de Larminat, who was away.

Meyer left that meeting with the distinct impression that the die was cast for the attack (*"l'impression tres nette que les jeux etaient faits, que Royan serait attaquée"*). This was January 2. Three days later, sleeping at Rochefort, he was awakened by the sound of airplanes flying south toward Royan. Those were the British Lancasters, three hundred and fifty of them, each carrying seven tons of bombs.

---

* This is Meyer's recollection of the conversation, in his chapter "Royan, Ville Détruite par erreur." Meyer tends to glorify his own activities in this book, but his account fits the other evidence.

** Three other pieces of evidence support Meyer's claim of German readiness to surrender:

A. A dispatch in *Samedi-Soir* in May, 1948 (reproduced in part in the Botton collection) tells a strange story which goes even further than Meyer. It reports, on the basis of a document it clams to have found in the Ministry of the Armed Forces, that a British agent, with the code name of "Aristede," parachuted into France to join the Resistance, reported later to his government in London that the Germans in the Royan area had offered to surrender if they would be given the honors of war, but that the French General Bertin said a surrender to the British would create a "diplomatic incident." This was, allegedly, September 8, 1944.

B. An open letter to General de Larminat by Dr. Veyssière Pierre, a former leader of the Royan Resistance (reproduced in the Botton collection) says: "Now we are sure that in August and September, 1944, the German high command—the commander of the fortress of Royan—made proposals of surrender that, if they had come about, would have prevented the worst; we know that on two occasions, he made contact with Colonel Cominetti, called Charly, commander of the Medoc groups; we know also that these attempts at negotiations were purely and simply repulsed by the French headquarters at Bordeaux, in order, no doubt, to add to the grandeur of military prestige."

C. The article of Paul Metadier (reprinted in a pamphlet, available in the library of Royan) in *La Lettre Medicale*, February 1948, gives Sir Samuel Hoare, former British Ambassador to France, as a source of the fact that the French military command had opposed the surrender of the German General to the British.

Meyer adds another piece of information: that about a month before the January 5 bombing, an American General, Commander of the Ninth Tactical Air Force, came to Cognac to offer the Southwest forces powerful bombing support, and suggested softening the Atlantic pockets by massive aerial bombardment. He proposed that since the Germans did not have aerial defenses for Royan, here were good targets for bomber-crew trainees in England. The French agreed, but insisted the targets be at two points which formed clear enclaves on the ocean, easily distinguishable from the city itself. No more was heard from the Americans, however, until the bombing itself.*

As it turned out, not trainees, but experienced pilots did the bombing, and Meyer concludes that even the American general (sent back to the U.S. after this, as a scapegoat, Meyer suggests) was not completely responsible.

Some blame devolved, he says, on the British Bomber Command, and some on the French generals, for not insisting on a point DeGaulle had made when he visited the area in September—that aerial attacks should only be undertaken here in coordination with ground assaults. Meyer concludes, however, that the real responsibility did not rest with the local military commanders. "To wipe out such a city is beyond military decision. It is a serious political act. It is impossible that the Supreme Command [he refers to Eisenhower and his staff] had not been at least consulted." In the event, he says, that the Allies are shocked by his accusations, they should open their military dossiers and, for the first time, reveal the truth.

If by January 1945 (despite von Rundstedt's Christmas counter-offensive in the Ardennes), it seemed clear that the Allies, well into France, and the Russians, having the Germans on the run, were on the way toward victory—then by April 1945 there was little doubt that the war was near its end. The Berlin radio announced on April 15 that the Russians and Americans were about to join forces around the Elbe, and

---

* This story appears also in Robert Aron's *Histoire de la Libération de la France*, June, 1944-May, 1945 (Librarie Artheme Fayard, 1959). Aron adds the point that the American general spent some time on this visit with and FFI (French Forces of the Interior) journalist who called the inhabitants of Royan "collaborators."

that two zones were being set up for a Germany cut in two. Nevertheless, a major land-air operation was launched April 14 against the Royan pocket, with over a thousand planes dropping bombs on a German force of 5,500 men, on a town containing at the time probably less than a thousand people.*

An article written in the summer of 1946 by a local writer commented on the mid-April assault:

> These last acts left great bitterness in the hearts of the Royannais, because the Armistice followed soon after, an Armistice foreseen by all. For the Royannais, this liberation by force was useless since Royan would have been, like La Rochelle, liberated normally some days later, without new damage, without new deaths, without new ruins. Only those who have visited Royan can give an account of the disaster. No report, no picture or drawing can convey it.

Another local person wrote:**

> Surely the destruction of Royan, on January 5, 1945, was an error and a crime: but what put the finishing touches on this folly was the final air raid on the ruins, on the buildings partially damaged, and on others remarkably spared on the periphery, with that infernal cargo of incendiary bombs. Thus was accomplished a deadly work of obvious uselessness, and thus was revealed to the world the powerful destructiveness of napalm.

The evidence seems overwhelming that factors of pride, military ambition, glory, honor were powerful motives in producing an unnecessary military operation. One of the local commanders wrote later: "It would have been more logical to wait for the surrender of Germany and thus to avoid

---

* Colle, *Royan, son passé, ses environs.* He reports the Germans, under Admiral Michahelles had 5,500 men, 150 cannon, four anti-aircraft batteries. They were well entrenched in concrete bunkers and surrounded by fields of land mines.

** "Les Préparatifs de l'Attaque" in Botton collection. The same writer claims (on the basis of a historical work by J. Mortin, *Au carrefour de l'Histoire*) that the formula for napalm was found in the eighteenth century by a Grenoblois goldsmith, who demonstrated it to the minister of war, after which Louis XV was so horrified he ordered the documents burned, saying that such a terrifying force must remain unknown for the good of man.

new human and material losses" but one could not "ignore important factors of morale" (*"faire abstraction de facteurs essentiels d'ordre moral"*).*

In 1947, a delegation of five leaders of Royan met with General de Larminat. After the war, the citizens of Royan had barred de Larminat from the town, in anger at the military operations under his command which had destroyed it, and at the widespread looting of the Royan homes by French soldiers after "liberation." He hoped now to persuade the Royannais that they had made a mistake. The meeting is described by Dr. Veyssière Pierre, former leader of the Resistance in Royan, and a holder of the Croix de Guerre, who says he hoped to get an explanation of the "useless sacrifice" of the population of the town, but "my self-deception was total, absolute." He quotes de Larminat saying the French military did not want the enemy "to surrender of his own accord; that would give the impression the Germans were unconquered."**

Another member of the French delegation, Dr. Domecq, a former Mayor and Resistance leader, responded to General de Larminat also:

> Royan was destroyed by mistake, you say, my general.... Those responsible have been punished, the order to attack, a few days before liberation, could not be questioned by the military.... The Germans had to feel our power! Permit me, my general, to tell you, once and for all, in the name of those who paid the cost: "La Victoire de Royan" does not exist, except for you.

General de Larminat responded to the criticism in the letter addressed to Paul Métadier.*** Pride and military ambition, he pointed

---

* *Revue Historique de l'armee*, January, 1946. An article in a regional journal after the war commented on those engaged in the April attacks: "Thanks to them, one could not say that the French army remained impotent before the German redoubts on the Atlantic wall." *Le Pays d'Ouest*, copy in the library at Royan.

** Open letter to General de Larminat, caustically addressing him as "Liberateur" de Royan. Reproduced in the Botton collection.

*** The exchange between Métadier and de Larminat is in a pamphlet in the possession of the library in Royan. The original Royan library was destroyed during the bombings, and in 1957, after twelve years, a new library was built.

out, were not sufficient explanations for such a huge operation; one had to seek a larger source: "This pride, this ambition, did not have the power to manufacture the shells which were used, to create the units which were sent, to divert the important aerial and naval forces that participated." De Larminat said that he had prepared the necessary plans for liquidating "*les poches d'Atlantique*" but that he did not judge the date. The date was fixed for him, and he executed the plans.

He ended his reply with an appeal to patriotism: "Must we therefore, throw opprobrium on old combatants because some isolated ones committed acts, unhappily inevitable in wartime? This is how it has been in all the wars of all time. No one ever, that I know, used this as a pretext to reduce the glory and the valour of the sacrifices made by the combatants." He spoke of the "simple, brave people" who will put "glory and national independence" before "material losses" and give "the respect due to those who fell, and for which many sacrificed their lives, to a patriotic ideal that the malcontents ("*les attentistes*") have always ignored."

Admiral Meyer, who is more sympathetic to de Larminat than most of the general's critics, had watched the attack on Royan from the heights of Medis, and described the scene:

> The weather was clear, the warmth oppressive. Under a fantastic concentration of fire, the enemy positions, the woods, and the ruins of Royan flamed. The countryside and the sky were thick with powder and yellow smoke. One could with difficulty distinguish the mutilated silhouette of the clock of Saint-Pierre, which burned like a torch. I knew that the allied planes were using for the first time, a new kind of incendiary explosive, a kind of jellied gasoline, known as napalm.

Larminat, he said, had good days and bad days, for in the evening after Royan was taken, and Meyer went to see the General: "He was visibly satisfied with having achieved this brilliant revenge.... Without saying that he was intoxicated with success, the General seemed to me however to have his appetite stimulated."

That exultation was felt at all levels. A press correspondent on the scene described the very heavy artillery bombardment which prepared the attack on the Royan area: 27,000 shells. Then the first aerial bombing on Saturday, April 14, with high explosives. Then the bombing all Sunday morning with napalm. By seven that evening they were in Royan. It was a blazing furnace. ("*La ville est un brasier.*") The next morning, they could still hear the clatter of machine guns in the woods nearby. Royan was still burning. ("*Royan brule encore.*") The dispatch ends: "It is a beautiful spring."

With Royan taken, they decided to attack the island of Oléron, opposite Rochefort. As Meyer says:

> The new victory had inflamed the passions of our soldiers, giving them the idea that nothing could resist them. News from the German front forecast a quick end to the war. Each one wanted a last moment to distinguish himself and get a bit of glory; moderation was scorned, prudence was seen as cowardice.

Meyer did not believe the attack on Oléron was necessary. But he participated assiduously in planning and executing it, happy to be once again involved in a naval operation, and convinced that his duty was only to carry out orders from above.

> The attack on Oléron was disputable from the point of view of general strategy. It was a costly luxury, a conquest without military value, on the eve of the war's end. But this was not for me to judge. My duty was limited to doing my best in making those military decisions which would fulfil my orders.

Meyer blames the political leaders above. Yet *blame* seems the wrong word, because Meyer believes it honorable to follow orders, whatever they are, against whatever adversary is chosen for him: "*Quant au soldat, depuis des millénaires, ce n'est plus lui qui forge ses armes et qui choisit son adversaire. Il n'a que le devoir d'obeir dans la pleine mesure de sa foi, de son courage, de sa resistance.*"*

---

* At one point, Meyer quotes Bismarck, who made German students write: "Man was not put in the world to be happy, but to do his duty!" In another frightening glimpse of what a well-trained military man of our century can believe, Meyer talks fondly of that special bond of the sea ("*une commune maitresse: la mer*") which unites sailors of different nations in their patriotic duty, and points, as an example of such laudable unity in action, to the landing of European troops in China in 1900 to crush the Boxer uprising.

One can see in the destruction of Royan that infinite chain of causes, that infinite dispersion of responsibility, which can give infinite work to historical scholarship and sociological speculation, and bring an infinitely pleasurable paralysis of the will. What a complex of motives! In the Supreme Allied Command, the simple momentum of the war, the pull of prior commitments and preparations, the need to fill out the circle, to pile up the victories as high as possible. At the local military level, the ambitions, petty and large, the tug of glory, the ardent need to participate in a grand communal effort by soldiers of all ranks. On the part of the American Air Force, the urge to try out a newly developed weapon. (Paul Métadier wrote: "In effect, the operation was above all characterized by the dropping of new incendiary bombs which the Air Force had just been supplied with. According to the famous formulation of one general: 'They were marvelous!'") And among all participants, high and low, French and American, the most powerful motive of all: The habit of obedience, the universal teaching of all cultures, not to get out of line, not even to think about that which one has not been assigned to think about, the negative motive of not having either a reason or a will to intercede.

Everyone can point, rightly, to someone else as being responsible. In that remarkable film *King and Country*, a simple-minded British country boy in the trenches of World War I walks away one day from the slaughter and is condemned to death in a two-step process where no one thinks he really should be executed but the officers in each step can blame those in the other. The original court sentences him to death thinking to make a strong point and then have the appeals tribunal overturn the verdict. The appeals board, upholding the verdict, can argue that the execution was not its decision. The man is shot. That procedure, one recalls, goes back to the Inquisition, when the church only conducted the trial, and the state carried out the execution, thus confusing both God and the people about the source of the decision.

More and more in our time, the mass production of massive evil requires an enormously complicated division of labor. No one is positively responsible for the horror that ensues. But every one is negatively responsible, because anyone can throw a wrench into the machinery. Not quite, of course—because only a few people have wrenches. The rest have only their hands and feet. That is, the power to interfere with the terrible progression is distributed unevenly, and therefore the sacrifice required varies, according to one's means. In that odd perversion of the natural which we call society (that is, nature seems to equip each species for its special needs) the greater one's capability for interference, the less urgent is the need to interfere.

It is the immediate victims—or tomorrow's—who have the greatest need, and the fewest wrenches. They must use their bodies (which may explain why rebellion is a rare phenomenon). This may suggest to those of us who have a bit more than our bare hands, and at least a small interest in stopping the machine, that we might play a peculiar role in breaking the social stalemate.

This may require resisting a false crusade—or refusing one or another expedition in a true one. But always, it means refusing to be transfixed by the actions of other people, the truths of other times. It means acting on what we feel and think, here, now, for human flesh and sense, against the abstractions of duty and obedience.

PART 7

Beyond Machiavellianism

19

Machiavellian Realism and U.S. Foreign Policy

While teaching courses in political theory at Boston Univeristy, and fascinated by the figure of Machiavelli, I came across the remarkable volume by Ralph Roeder, *The Man of the Rennaisance*, with its brilliant portraits of the dissident Savonarola and the toady Machiavelli. At the same time I noted the respect with which Machiavelli was treated by people on all parts of the political spectrum. The Vietnam War led many people, including myself, to look more closely at the history of United States foreign policy, and to me there was a distinct Machiavellian thread running through that history. This essay appeared in my book *Declarations of Independence* (HarperCollins, 1991).

Interests: The Prince and the Citizen

About 500 years ago modern political thinking began. Its enticing surface was the idea of "realism." Its ruthless center was the idea that with a worthwhile end one could justify any means. Its spokesman was Nicolo Machiavelli.

In the year 1498 Machiavelli became adviser on foreign and military affairs to the government of Florence, one of the great Italian cities of that time. After fourteen years of service, a change of government led to his dismissal, and he spent the rest of his life in exile in the countryside outside of Florence. During that time he wrote, among other things, a little book called *The Prince*, which became the world's most famous handbook of political wisdom for governments and their advisers.

Four weeks before Machiavelli took office, something happened in Florence that made a profound impression on him. It was a public hanging. The victim was a monk named Savonarola, who preached that people could be guided by their "natural reason." This threatened to diminish the importance of the Church fathers, who then showed their importance by having Savonarola arrested. His hands were bound behind his back and he was taken through the streets in the night, the crowds swinging lanterns near his face, peering for the signs of his dangerousness.

Savonarola was interrogated and tortured for ten days. They wanted to extract a confession, but he was stubborn. The Pope, who kept in touch with the torturers, complained that they were not getting results quickly enough. Finally the right words came, and Savonarola was sentenced to death. As his body swung in the air, boys from the neighborhood stoned it. The corpse was set afire, and when the fire had done its work, the ashes were strewn in the river Arno.

In *The Prince*, Machiavelli refers to Savonarola and says, "Thus it comes about that all armed prophets have conquered and unarmed ones failed."

Political ideas are centered on the issue of *ends* (What kind of society do we want?) and *means* (How will we get it?). In that one sentence about unarmed prophets Machiavelli settled for modern governments the question of ends: conquest. And the question of means: force.

Machiavelli refused to be deflected by utopian dreams or romantic hopes and by questions of right and wrong or good and bad. He is the father of modern political realism, or what has been called *realpolitik:* "It appears to me more proper to go to the truth of the matter than to its imagination...for how we live is so far removed from how we ought to live, that he who abandons what is done for what ought to be done, will rather learn to bring about his own ruin than his preservation."

It is one of the most seductive ideas of our time. We hear on all sides the cry of "be realistic...you're living in the real world," from political platforms, in the press, and at home. The insistence on building more nuclear weapons, when we already possess more than enough to destroy the world, is based on "realism." The *Wall Street Journal*, approving a Washington, D.C., ordinance allowing the police to arrest any person on the street refusing to move on when ordered, wrote, "D.C.'s action is born of living in the real world." And consider how often a parent (usually a father) has said to a son or daughter: "It's good to have idealistic visions of a better world, but you're living in the real world, so act accordingly."

How many times have the dreams of young people—the desire to help others; to devote their lives to the sick or the poor; or to poetry, music, or drama—been demeaned as foolish romanticism, impractical in a world where one must "make a living"? Indeed, the economic system reinforces the same idea by rewarding those who spend their lives on "practical" pursuits—while making life difficult for the artist, poets, nurses, teachers, and social workers.

Realism is seductive because once you have accepted the reasonable notion that you should base your actions on reality, you are too often led to accept, without much questioning, someone else's version of what that reality is. It is a crucial act of independent thinking to be skeptical of someone else's description of reality.

When Machiavelli claims to "go to the truth of the matter," he is making the frequent claim of important people (writers, political leaders) who press their ideas on others: that their account is "the truth," that they are being "objective."

But his reality may not be our reality; his truth may not be our truth. The real world is infinitely complex. Any description of it must be a partial description, so a choice is made about what part of reality to describe, and behind that choice is often a definite interest, in the sense of something useful for a particular individual or group. Behind the claim of someone giving us an objective picture of the real world is the assumption that we all have the same interests, and so we can trust the one who describes the world for us, because that person has our interests at heart.

It is very important to know if our interests are the same, because a description is never simply neutral and innocent; it has consequences. No description is merely that. Every description is in some way a prescription. If you describe human nature as Machiavelli does, as basically immoral, it suggests that it is realistic, indeed only human, that you should behave that way too.

The notion that all our interests are the same (the political leaders and the citizens, the millionaire and the homeless person) deceives us. It is a deception useful to those who run modern societies, where the support of the population is necessary for the smooth operation of the machinery of everyday life and the perpetuation of the present arrangements of wealth and power.

When the Founding Fathers of the United States wrote the Preamble to the Constitution, their first words were, "We the People of the United States, in order to form a more perfect union, establish justice..." The Constitution thus looked as if it were written by all the people, representing their interests.

In fact, the Constitution was drawn up by fifty-five men, all white and mostly rich, who represented a certain elite group in the new nation. The document itself accepted slavery as legitimate, and at that time about one of every five persons in the population was a black slave. The conflicts between rich and poor and black and white, the dozens of riots and rebellions in the century before the Revolution, and a major uprising in western Massachusetts just before the convening of the Constitutional Convention (Shays' Rebellion) were all covered over by the phrase "We the people."

Machiavelli did not pretend to a common interest. He talked about what "is necessary for a prince." He dedicated *The Prince* to the rich and powerful Lorenzo di Medici, whose family ruled Florence and included popes and monarchs. (*The Columbia Encyclopedia* has this intriguing description of the Medici: "The genealogy of the family is complicated by the numerous illegitimate offspring and by the tendency of some of the members to dispose of each other by assassination.")

In exile, writing his handbook of advice for the Medici, Machiavelli ached to be called back to the city to take his place in the inner circle. He wanted nothing more than to serve the prince.

In our time we find greater hypocrisy. Our Machiavellis, our presidential advisers, our assistants for national security, and our secretaries of state insist they serve "the national interest," "national security," and "national defense." These phrases put everyone in the country under one enormous blanket, camouflaging the differences between the interest of those who run the government and the interest of the average citizen.

The American Declaration of Independence, however, clearly understood that difference of interest between government and citizen. It says that the purpose of government is to secure certain rights for its citizens—life, liberty, equality, and the pursuit of happiness. But governments may not fulfill these purposes and so "whenever any form of government becomes destructive of these ends, it is the right of the people to alter or abolish it, and to institute new government."

The end of Machiavelli's *The Prince* is clearly different. It is not the welfare of the citizenry, but national power, conquest, and control. All is done in order "to maintain the state."

In the United States today, the Declaration of Independence hangs on schoolroom walls, but foreign policy follows Machiavelli. Our language is more deceptive than his; the purpose of foreign policy, our leaders say, is to serve the "national interest," fulfill our "world responsibility." In 1986 General William Westmoreland said that during World War II the United States "inherited the mantle of leadership of the free world" and "became the international champions of liberty." This, from the man who, as chief of military operations in the Vietnam War, conducted a brutal campaign that resulted in the deaths of hundreds of thousands of Vietnamese noncombatants.

Sometimes, the language is more direct, as when President Lyndon

Johnson, speaking to the nation during the Vietnam War, talked of the
United States as being "number one." Or, when he said, "Make no mistake about it, we will prevail."

Even more blunt was a 1980 article in the influential *Foreign Affairs*
by Johns Hopkins political scientist Robert W. Tucker; in regard to
Central America, he wrote, "We have regularly played a determining role
in making and in unmaking governments, and we have defined what we
have considered to be the acceptable behavior of governments." Tucker
urged "a policy of a resurgent America to prevent the coming to power of
radical regimes in Central America" and asked, "Would a return to a policy of the past work in Central America?... There is no persuasive reason
for believing it would not... Right-wing governments will have to be
given steady outside support, even, if necessary, by sending in American
forces."

Tucker's suggestion became the Central America policy of the Reagan
administration, as it came into office in early 1981. His "sending in
American forces" was too drastic a step for an American public that clearly opposed another Vietnam (unless done on a small scale, like Reagan's
invasion of Grenada, and Bush's invasion of Panama). But for the following eight years, the aims of the United States were clear; to overthrow
the left-wing government of Nicaragua and to keep in place the right-
wing government of El Salvador.

Two Americans who visited El Salvador in 1983 for the New York
City Bar Association described for *The New York Times* a massacre of
eighteen peasants by local troops in Sonsonate province:

> Ten military advisers are attached to the Sonsonate armed forces.. The
> episode contains all the unchanging elements of the Salvadoran tragedy—
> uncontrolled military violence against civilians, the apparent ability of the
> wealthy to procure official violence...and the presence of United States mil-
> itary advisers, working with the Salvadoran military responsible for these
> monstrous practices...after 30,000 unpunished murders by security and
> military forces and over 10,000 "disappearances" of civilians in custody,
> the root causes of the killings remain in place, and the killing goes on.

The purpose of its policy in Central America, said the U.S. government, was to protect the country from the Soviet threat: a Soviet base in Nicaragua and a possible Soviet base in El Salvador. This was not quite believable. Was the Soviet Union prepared to launch an invasion of the United States from Central America? Was a nation that could not win a war on its borders with Afghanistan going to send an army across the Atlantic Ocean to Nicaragua? And what then? Would that army then march up through Honduras into Guatemala, then through all of Mexico, into Texas, and then...?

It was as absurd as the domino theory of the Vietnam War, in which the falling dominos of Southeast Asia would have had to swim the Pacific to get to San Francisco. Did the Soviet Union, with intercontinental ballistic missiles, with submarines off the coast of Long Island, need Central America as a base for attacking the United States?

Nevertheless, the Kissinger Commission, set up by President Reagan to advise him on Central American policy, warned in its report that our "southern flank" was in danger—a biological reference designed to make all of us nervous.

Even a brief look at history was enough to make one skeptical. How could we explain our frequent interventions in Central America *before* 1917, before the Bolshevik Revolution? How could we explain our taking control of Cuba and Puerto Rico in 1898; our seizure of the Canal Zone in 1903; our dispatch of marines to Honduras, Nicaragua, Panama, and Guatemala in the early 1900s; our bombardment of a Mexican town in 1914; and our long military occupation of Haiti and the Dominican Republic starting in 1915 and 1916? All this before the Soviet Union existed.

There was another official reason given for U.S. intervention in Central America in the 1980s: to "restore democracy." This, too, was hardly believable. Throughout the period after World War II our government had supported undemocratic governments, indeed vicious military dictatorships; in Batista's Cuba, Somoza's Nicaragua, Armas's Guatemala, Pinoche's Chile, and Duvalier's Haiti as well as in El Salvador and other countries of Latin America.

The actual purpose of U.S. policy in Central America was expressed by Tucker in the most clear Machiavellian terms: "The great object of American foreign policy ought to be the restoration of a more normal political world, a world in which those states possessing the elements of great power once again play the role their power entitles them to play."

Undoubtedly, there are Americans who respond favorably to this idea, that the United States should be a "great power" in the world, should dominate other countries, should be number one. Perhaps the assumption is that our domination is benign and that our power is used for kindly purposes. The history of our relations with Latin America does not suggest this. Besides, is it really in keeping with the American ideal of equality of all peoples to insist that we have the right to control the affairs of other countries? Are we the only country entitled to a Declaration of Independence?

Means: The Lion and the Fox

There should be clues to the rightness of the ends we pursue by examining the means we use to achieve those ends. I am assuming there is always some connection between ends and means. All means become ends in the sense that they have immediate consequences apart from the ends they are supposed to achieve. And all ends are themselves means to other ends. Was there not a link, for Machiavelli, between his crass end—power for the prince—and the various means he found acceptable?

For a year Machiavelli was ambassador to Cesare Borgia, conqueror of Rome. He describes one event that "is worthy of note and of imitation by others." Rome had been disorderly, and Cesare Borgia decided he needed to make the people "peaceful and obedient to his rule." Therefore, "he appointed Messer Remirro de Orco, a cruel and able man, to whom he gave the fullest authority" and who, in a short time, made Rome "orderly and united." But Cesare Borgia knew his policies had aroused hatred, so, in order to purge the minds of the people and to win them over completely, he resolved to show that if any cruelty had taken place it was not by his orders, but through the harsh disposition of his minister. And having found the opportunity he had him cut in half and placed one morning in the public square at Cesena with a piece of wood and blood-stained knife by his side.

In recent American history, we have become familiar with the technique of rulers letting subordinates do the dirty work, which they can later disclaim. As a result of the Watergate scandals in the Nixon administration (a series of crimes committed by underlings in his behalf), a number of his people (former CIA agents, White House aides, and even the attorney-general) were sent to prison. But Nixon himself, although he was forced to resign his office, escaped criminal prosecution, arranging to be pardoned when his vice-president, Gerald Ford, became president. Nixon retired in prosperity and, in a few years, became a kind of elder statesman, a Godfather of politics, looked to for sage advice.

Perhaps as a way of calming the public in that heated time of disillusionment with the government because of Vietnam and Watergate, a Senate committee in 1974-1975 conducted an investigation of the intelligence agencies. It discovered that the CIA and the FBI had violated the law countless times (opening mail, breaking into homes and offices, etc.). In the course of that investigation, it was also revealed that the CIA, going back to the Kennedy administration, had plotted the assassination of a number of foreign rulers, including Cuba's Fidel Castro. But the president himself, who clearly was in favor of such actions, was not to be directly involved, so that he could deny knowledge of it. This was given the term *plausible denial.*

As the committee reported:

Non-attribution to the United States for covert operations was the original and principal purpose of the so-called doctrine of "plausible denial." Evidence before the Committee clearly demonstrates that this concept, designed to protect the United States and its operatives from the consequences of disclosures, has been expanded to mask decisions of the president and his senior staff members.

In 1988, a story in a Beirut magazine led to information that Ronald Reagan's administration had been secretly selling arms to Iran, the declared enemy of the United States, and using the proceeds to give military aid to counterrevolutionaries (the "contras") in Nicaragua, thus violating an act passed by Congress. Reagan and Vice President Bush denied involvement, although the evidence pointed very strongly to their participation. Instead of impeaching them, however, congress put their emissaries on the witness stand, and later several of them were indicted. One of them (Robert McFarland) tried to commit suicide. Another, Colonel Oliver North, stood trial for lying to Congress, was found guilty, but was not sentenced to prison. Reagan was not compelled to testify about what he had done. He retired in peace and Bush became the next president of the United States, both beneficiaries of plausible denial. Machiavelli would have admired the operation.

A prince, Machiavelli suggested, should emulate both the lion and the fox. The lion uses force. "The character of peoples varies, and it is easy to persuade them of a thing, but difficult to keep them in that persuasion. And so it is necessary to order things so that when they no longer believe, they can be made to believe by force... Fortune is a woman, and it is necessary, if you wish to master her, to conquer her by force." The fox uses deception.

> If all men were good, this would not be good advice, but since they are dishonest and do not keep faith with you, you, in return, need not keep faith with them; and no prince was ever at a loss for plausible reasons to cloak a breach of faith... The experience of our times shows those princes to have done great things who have had little regard for good faith, and have been able by astuteness to confuse men's brains.

This advice for the prince has been followed in our time by all sorts of dictators and generalissimos. Hitler kept a copy of *The Prince* at his bedside, it is said. (Who says? How do they know?) Mussolini used Machiavelli for his doctoral dissertation. Lenin and Stalin are also supposed to have read Machiavelli. Certainly the Italian Communist Gramsci wrote favorably about Machiavelli, claiming that Machiavelli was not really giving advice to princes, who knew all that already, but to "those who do not know," thus educating "those who must recognize certain necessary means, even if those of tyrants, because they want certain ends."

The prime ministers and presidents of modern democratic states, despite their pretensions, have also admired and followed Machiavelli. Max Lerner, a prominent liberal commentator on the post-World War II period, in his introduction to Machiavelli's writings, says of him: "The common meaning he has for democrats and dictators alike is that, whatever your ends, you must be clear-eyed and unsentimental in pursuit of them." Lerner finds in Machiavelli's *Discourses* that one of his important ideas is "the need in the conduct even of a democratic state for the will to survive and therefore for ruthless instead of half-hearted measures."

Thus the democratic state, behaving like the lion, uses force when persuasion does not work. It uses it against its own citizens when they cannot be persuaded to obey the laws. It uses it against other peoples in the act of war, not always in self-defense, but often when it cannot persuade other nations to do its bidding.

For example, at the start of the twentieth century, although Colombia was willing to sell the rights to the Panama Canal to the United States, it wanted more money than the United States was willing to pay. So the warships were sent on their way, a little revolution was instigated in Panama, and soon the Canal Zone was in the hands of the United States. As one U.S. Senator described the operation, "We stole it fair and square."

The modern liberal state, like Machiavelli's fox, often uses deception to gain its ends—not so much deception of the foreign enemy (which, after all, has little faith in its adversaries), but of its own citizens, who have been taught to trust their leaders.

One of the important biographies of President Franklin D. Roosevelt is titled *Roosevelt: The Lion and the Fox*. Roosevelt deceived the American public at the start of World War II, in September and October 1941, misstating the facts about two instances involving German submarines and American destroyers (claiming the destroyer *Greer*, which was attacked by a German submarine, was on an innocent mission when in fact it was tracking the sub for the British Navy). A historian sympathetic to him wrote, "Franklin Roosevelt repeatedly deceived the American people during the period before Pearl Harbor.... He was like the physician who must tell the patient lies for the patient's own good."

Then there were the lies of President John Kennedy and Secretary of State Dean Rusk when they told the public the United States was not responsible for the 1961 invasion of Cuba, although in fact the invasion had been organized by the CIA.

The escalation of the war in Vietnam started with a set of lies—in August 1964—about incidents in the Gulf of Tonkin. The United States announced two "unprovoked" attacks on U.S. destroyers by North Vietnamese boats. One of them almost certainly did not take place. The other was undoubtedly provoked by the proximity (ten miles) of the destroyer to the Vietnamese coast and by a series of CIA-organized raids on the coast.

The lies then multiplied. One of them was President Johnson's statement that the U.S. Air Force was only bombing "military targets." Another was a deception by President Richard Nixon; he concealed from the American public the 1969-1970 massive bombing of Cambodia, a country with which we were supposed to be at peace.

The Advisers

Advisers and assistants to presidents, however committed they are in their rhetoric to the values of modern liberalism, have again and again participated in acts of deception that would have brought praise from Machiavelli. His goal was to serve the prince and national power. So was theirs. Because they were advisers to a liberal democratic state, they assumed that advancing the power of such a state was a moral end, which then justified both force and deception. But cannot a liberal state carry out immoral policies? Then the adviser (deceiving himself this time) would consider that his closeness to the highest circles of power put him in a position to affect, even reverse, such policies.

It was a contemporary of Machiavelli, Thomas More, who warned intellectuals about being trapped into service to the state and about the self-deception in which the adviser believes he will be a good influence in the higher councils of the government. In More's book *Utopia*, spokesperson Raphael is offered the advice commonly given today to young people who want to be social critics, prodding the government from outside, like Martin Luther King or Ralph Nader. The advice is to get on the *inside*. Raphael is told, "I still think that if you could overcome the aversion you have to the courts of princes, you might do a great deal of good to mankind by the advice that you would give."

Raphael replies, "If I were at the court of some king and proposed wise laws to him and tried to root out of him the dangerous seeds of evil, do you not think I would either be thrown out of his court or held in scorn?" He goes on,

> Imagine me at the court of the King of France. Suppose I were sitting in his council with the King himself presiding, and that the wisest men were earnestly discussing by what methods and intrigues the King might keep Milan, recover Naples so often lost, then overthrow the Venetians and subdue all Italy, and add Flanders, Brabant, and even all Burgundy to his realm, besides some other nations he had planned to invade. Now in all this great ferment, with so many brilliant men planning together how to carry on war, imagine so modest a man as myself standing up and urging them to change all their plans.

More might have been describing the historian Arthur Schlesinger, Jr., adviser to President Kennedy, who thought it was "a terrible idea" to go ahead with the CIA Bay of Pigs invasion of Cuba in 1961, two years after the revolution there. But he did not raise his voice in protest, because, as he later admitted, he was intimidated by the presence of "such august figures as the Secretaries of State and Defense and the Joint Chiefs of Staff." He wrote, "In the months after the Bay of Pigs I bitterly reproached myself for having kept so silent during those crucial discussions in the Cabinet room."

But the intimidation of Schlesinger-as-adviser went beyond silencing him in the cabinet room—it led him to produce a nine-page memorandum to President Kennedy, written shortly before the invasion of Cuba, in which he is as blunt as Machiavelli himself in urging deception of the public to conceal the U.S. role in the invasion. This would be necessary because "a great many people simply do not at this moment see that Cuba presents so grave and compelling a threat to our national security as to justify a course of action which much of the world will interpret as calculated aggression against a small nation."

The memorandum goes on, "The character and repute of President Kennedy constitute one of our greatest national resources. Nothing should be done to jeopardize this invaluable asset. When lies must be told, they should be told by subordinate officials." It goes on to suggest "that someone other than the President make the final decision and do so in his absence—someone whose head can later be placed on the block if things go terribly wrong." (Cesare Borgia again, only lacking the bloodstained knife.)

Schlesinger included in his memo sample questions and lying answers in case the issue of the invasion came up in a press conference:

> Q. Mr. President, is CIA involved in this affair?
> A. I can assure you that the United States has no intention of using force to overthrow the Castro regime.

The scenario was followed. Four days before the invasion President Kennedy told a press conference, "There will not be, under any conditions, any intervention in Cuba by U.S. armed forces."

Schlesinger was just one of dozens of presidential advisers who behaved like little Machiavellis in the years when revolutions in Vietnam and Latin America brought hysterical responses on the part of the U.S. government. These intellectuals could see no better role for themselves than to serve national power.

Kissinger, secretary of state to Nixon, did not even have the mild qualms of Schlesinger. He surrendered himself with ease to the princes of war and destruction. In private discussions with old colleagues from Harvard who thought the Vietnam War immoral, he presented himself as someone trying to bring it to an end, but in his official capacity he was the willing intellectual tool of a policy that involved the massive killing of civilians in Vietnam.

Kissinger approved the bombing and invasion of Cambodia, an act so disruptive of the delicate Cambodian society that it can be considered an important factor in the rise of the murderous Pol Pot regime in that country. After he and the representatives of North Vietnam had negotiated a peace agreement to end the war in late 1972, he approved the breaking off of the talks and the brutal bombardment of residential districts in Hanoi by the most ferocious bombing plane of the time, the B52.

Kissinger's biographers describe his role: "If he had disapproved of Nixon's policy, he could have argued against the Cambodia attack. But there is no sign that he ever mustered his considerable influence to persuade the president to hold his fire. Or that he ever considered resigning in protest. Quite the contrary, Kissinger supported the policy."

During the Christmas 1972 bombings *New York Times* columnist James Reston wrote,

> It may be and probably is true, that Mr. Kissinger as well as Secretary of State Rogers and most of the senior officers in the State Department are opposed to the President's bombing offensive in North Vietnam.. But Mr. Kissinger is too much a scholar, with too good a sense of humor and history, to put his own thoughts ahead of the president's.

It seems that journalists too, can be Machiavellian.

Serving National Powers

Machiavelli never questioned that national power and the position of the prince were proper ends: "And it must be understood that a prince...cannot observe all those things which are considered good in men, being often obliged, in order to maintain the state, to act against faith, against charity, against humanity, and against religion."

The end of national power may be beneficial to the prince, and even to the prince's advisers, an ambitious lot. But why should it be assumed as a good end for the average citizen? Why should the citizen tie his or her fate to the nation-state, which is perfectly willing to sacrifice the lives and liberties of its own citizens for the power, the profit, and the glory of politicians or corporate executives or generals?

For a prince, a dictator, or a tyrant national power is an end unquestioned. A democratic state, however, substituting an elected president for a prince, must present national power as benign, serving the interests of liberty, justice, and humanity. If such a state, which is surrounded with the rhetoric of democracy and liberty and, in truth, has some measure of both, engages in a war that is clearly against a vicious and demonstrably evil enemy, then the end seems so clean and clear that any means to defeat that enemy may seem justified.

Such a state was the United States and such an enemy was fascism, represented by Germany, Italy, and Japan. Therefore, when the atomic bomb appeared to be the means for a quicker victory, there was little hesitation to use it.

Very few of us can imagine ourselves as presidential advisers, having to deal with their moral dilemmas (if, indeed, they retain enough integrity to consider them dilemmas). It is much easier, I think, for average citizens to see themselves in the position of the scientists who were secretly assembled in New Mexico during World War II to make the atomic bomb. We may be able to imagine our own trade or profession, our particular skills, called on to serve the policies of the nation. The scientists who served Hitler, like the rocket expert Werner von Braun, could be as cool as Machiavelli in their subservience; they would serve national power without asking questions. They were professionals, totally consumed with doing "a good job" and they would do that job for whoever happened to be in power. So, when Hitler was defeated and von Braun was brought by military intelligence agents to the United States, he cheerfully went ahead and worked on rockets for the United States, as he had done for Hitler.

As one satirical songwriter put it:

Once the rockets are up,
Who cares where they come down?
That's not our department,
Says Werner von Braun.

The scientists who worked on the Manhattan Project were not like that. One cannot imagine them turning to Hitler and working for him if he were victorious. They were conscious, in varying degrees, that this was a war against fascism and that it was invested with a powerful moral cause. Therefore, to build this incredibly powerful weapon was to use a terrible means, but for a noble end.

And yet there was one element these scientists had in common with Werner von Braun: the sheer pleasure of doing a job well, of professional competence, and of scientific discovery, all of which could make one forget, or at least put in the background, the question of human consequences.

After the war, when the making of a thermonuclear bomb was proposed, a bomb a thousand times more destructive that the one dropped on Hiroshima, J. Robert Oppenheimer, personally horrified by the idea, was still moved to pronounce the scheme of Edward Teller and Stanislaw Ulam for producing it as "technically sweet." Teller, defending the project against scientists who saw it as genocidal, said, "The important thing in any science is to do the things that can be done." And, whatever Enrico Fermi's moral scruples were (he was one of the top scientists in the Manhattan Project), he pronounced the plan for making the bombs "superb physics."

Robert Jungk, a German researcher who interviewed many of the scientists involved in the making of the bomb, tried to understand their lack of resistance to dropping the bomb on Hiroshima. "They felt themselves caught in a vast machinery and they certainly were inadequately informed as to the true political and strategic situation." But he does not excuse their inaction. "If at any time they had had the moral strength to protest on purely humane grounds against the dropping of the bomb, their attitude would no doubt have deeply impressed the president, the Cabinet and the generals."

Using the atomic bombs on populated cities was justified in moral terms by American political leaders. Henry Stimson, whose Interim Committee had the job of deciding whether or not to use the atomic bomb, said later it was done "to end the war in victory with the least possible cost in the lives of the men in the armies." This was based on the assumption that without atomic bombs, an invasion of Japan would be necessary, which would cost many American lives.

It was a morality limited by nationalism, perhaps even racism. The saving of American lives was considered far more important than the saving of Japanese lives. Numbers were wildly thrown into the air (for example, Secretary of State James Byrnes talked of "a million casualties" resulting from an invasion), but there was no attempt to seriously estimate American casualties and weigh that against the consequences for Japanese men and women, old people and babies. (The closest to such an attempt was a military estimate that an invasion of the southernmost island of Japan would cause 30,000 American dead and wounded.)

The evidence today is overwhelming that an invasion of Japan was not necessary to bring the war to an end. Japan was defeated, in disarray, and ready to surrender. The U.S. Strategic Bombing Survey, which interviewed 700 Japanese military and political officials after the war, came to this conclusion:

> Based on a detailed investigation of all the facts and supported by the testimony of the surviving Japanese leaders involved, it is the Survey's opinion that certainly prior to 31 December 1945, and in all probability prior to 1 November 1945, Japan would have surrendered even if the atomic bombs had not been dropped, even if Russia had not entered the war, and even if no invasion had been planned or contemplated.

After the war American scholar Robert Butow went through the papers of the Japanese Ministry of Foreign Affairs, the records of the International Military Tribunal of the Far East (which tried Japanese leaders as war criminals), and the interrogation files of the U.S. Army. He also interviewed many of the Japanese principals and came to this conclusion: "Had the Allies given the Prince (Prince Konoye, special emissary to Moscow, who was working on Russian intercession for peace) a week of grace in which to obtain his Government's support for the acceptance of the proposals, the war might have ended toward the latter part of July or the very beginning of the month of August, without the atomic bomb and without Soviet participation in the conflict."

On July 13, 1945, three days before the successful explosion of the first atomic bomb in New Mexico, the United States intercepted Japanese Foreign Minister Togo's secret cable to Ambassador Sato in Moscow, asking that he get the Soviets to intercede and indicating that Japan was ready to end the war, so long as it was not unconditional surrender.

On August 2, the Japanese foreign office sent a message to the Japanese ambassador in Moscow, "There are only a few days left in which to make arrangements to end the war.. As for the definite terms... it is our intention to make the Potsdam Three-Power Declaration [which called for unconditional surrender] the basis of the study regarding these terms."

Barton Bernstein, a Stanford historian who has studied the official documents closely, wrote,

> This message, like earlier ones, was probably intercepted by American intelligence and decoded. It had no effect on American policy. There is not evidence that the message was sent to Truman and Byrnes [secretary of state], nor any evidence that they followed the intercepted messages during the Potsdam conference. They were unwilling to take risks in order to save Japanese lives.

In his detailed and eloquent history of the making of the bomb, Richard Rhodes says, "The bombs were authorized not because the

Japanese refused to surrender but because they refused to surrender unconditionally."

The one condition necessary for Japan to end the war was an agreement to maintain the sanctity of the Japanese emperor, who was a holy figure to the Japanese people. Former ambassador to Japan Joseph Grew, based on his knowledge of Japanese culture, had been trying to persuade the U.S. government of the importance of allowing the emperor to remain in place.

Herbert Feis, who had unique access to State Department files and the records on the Manhattan Project, noted that in the end the United States did give the assurances the Japanese wanted on the emperor. He writes, "The curious mind lingers over the reasons why the American government waited so long before offering the Japanese those various assurances which it did extend later."

Why was the United States in a rush to drop the bomb, if the reason of saving lives turns out to be empty, if the probability was that the Japanese would have surrendered even without an invasion? Historian Gar Alperovitz, after going through the papers of the American officials closest to Truman and most influential in the final decision, and especially the diaries of Henry Stimson, concludes that the atomic bombs were dropped to impress the Soviet Union, as a first act in establishing American power in the postwar world. He points out that the Soviet Union had promised to enter the war against Japan on August 8. The bomb was dropped on August 6.

The scientist Leo Szilard had met with Truman's main policy adviser in May 1945 and reported later: "Byrnes did not argue that it was necessary to use the bomb against the cities of Japan in order to win the war.. Mr. Byrnes' view was that our possessing and demonstrating the bomb would make Russia more manageable."

The *end* of dropping the bomb seems, from the evidence, to have been not winning the war, which was already assured, not saving lives, for it was highly probably no American invasion would be necessary, but the aggrandizement of American national power at the moment and in the postwar period. For this end, the means were among the most awful yet devised by human beings—burning people alive, maiming them horribly, and leaving them with radiation sickness, which would kill them slowly and with great pain.

I remember my junior-high-school social studies teacher telling the class that the difference between a democracy like the United States and the "totalitarian states" was the "they believe that the end justifies any means, and we do not." But this was before Hiroshima and Nagasaki.

To make a proper moral judgment, we would have to put into the balancing the testimony of the victims. Here are the words of three survivors, which would have to be multiplied by tens of thousands to gie a fuller picture.

A thirty-five-year-old man: "A woman with her jaw missing and her tongue hanging out of her mouth was wandering around the area of Shinsho-machi in the heavy, black rain. She was heading toward the north crying for help."

A seventeen-year-old girl: "I walked past Hiroshima Station...and saw people with their bowels and brains coming out.... I saw an old lady carrying a suckling infant in her arms...I saw many children...with dead mothers...I just cannot put into words the horror I felt."

A fifth-grade girl: "Everybody in the shelter was crying out loud. Those voices...they aren't cries, they are moans that penetrate to the marrow of your bones and make your hair stand on end... I do not know how many times I called begging that they would cut off my burned arms and legs."

In the summer of 1966 my wife and I were invited to an international gathering in Hiroshima to commemorate the dropping of the bomb and to dedicate ourselves to a world free of warfare. On the morning of August 6, tens of thousands of people gathered in a park in Hiroshima and stood in total, almost unbearable, silence, awaiting the exact moment—8:16 AM—when on August 6, 1945, the bomb had been dropped. When the moment came, the silence was broken by a sudden roaring sound in the air, eerie and frightening until we realized it was the sound of the beating of wings of thousands of doves, which had been released at that moment to declare the aim of a peaceful world.

A few days later, some of us were invited to a house in Hiroshima that had been established as a center for victims of the bomb to spend time with one another and discuss common problems. We were asked to speak to the group. When my turn came, I stood up and felt I must get something off my conscience. I wanted to say that I had been an air force bombardier in Europe, that I had dropped bombs that killed and maimed people, and that until this moment I had not seen the human results of such bombs, and that I was ashamed of what I had done and wanted to help make sure things like that never happened again.

I never got the words out, because as I started to speak I looked out at the Japanese men and women sitting on the floor in front of me, without arms, or without legs, but all quietly waiting for me to speak. I choked on my words, could not say anything for a moment, fighting for control, finally managed to thank them for inviting me and sat down.

For the idea that any means—mass murder, the misuse of science, the corruption of professionalism—are acceptable to achieve the end of national power, the ultimate example of our time is Hiroshima. For us, as citizens, the experience of Hiroshima and Nagasaki suggests that we reject Machiavelli, that we do not accept subservience, whether to princes or presidents, and that we examine for ourselves the ends of public policy to determine whose interests they really serve. We must examine the means used to achieve those ends to decide if they are compatible with equal justice for all human beings on earth.

The Anti-Machiavellians

There have always been people who did things for themselves, against the dominant ideology, and when there were enough of them history had its splendid moments: a war was called to a halt, a tyrant was overthrown, an enslaved people won its freedom, the poor won a small victory. Even some people close to the circles of power, in the fade of overwhelming pressure to conform have summoned the moral strength to dissent, ignoring the Machiavellian advice to leave the end unquestioned and the means unexamined.

Not all the atomic scientists rushed into the excitement of building the bomb. When Oppenheimer was recruiting for the project, as he later told the Atomic Energy Commission, most people accepted. "This sense of excitement, of devotion and of patriotism in the end prevailed." However, the physicist I.I. Rabi, asked by Oppenheimer to be his associate director at Los Alamos, refused to join. He was heavily involved in developing radar, which he thought important for the war, but he found it abhorrent, as Oppenheimer reported, that "the culmination of three centuries of physics" should be a weapon of mass destruction.

Just before the bomb was tested and used, Rabi worried about the role of scientists in war:

> If we take the stand that our object is merely to see that the next war is bigger and better, we will ultimately lose the respect of the public.... We will become the unpaid servants of the munitions makers and mere technicians rather than the self-sacrificing public-spirited citizens which we feel ourselves to be.

Nobel Prize-winning physical chemist James Franck, working with the University of Chicago metallurgical laboratory on problems of building the bomb, headed a committee on social and political implications of the new weapon. In June 1945, the Franck Committee wrote a report advising against a surprise atomic bombing of Japan: "If we consider international agreement on total prevention of nuclear warfare as a paramount objective...this kind of introduction of atomic weapons to the world may easily destroy all our chances of success." Dropping the bomb "will mean a flying start toward an unlimited armaments race," the report said.

The committee went to Washington to deliver the report personally to Henry Stimson, but were told, falsely, that he was out of the city. Neither Stimson nor the scientific panel advising him was in a mood to accept the argument of the Franck Report.

Scientist Leo Szilard, who had been responsible for the letter from Albert Einstein to Franklin Roosevelt suggesting a project to develop an atomic bomb, also fought a hard but futile battle against the bomb being dropped on a Japanese city. The same month that the bomb was successfully tested in New Mexico, July 1945, Szilard circulated a petition among the scientists, protesting in advance against the dropping of the bomb, arguing that "a nation which sets the precedent of using these newly liberated forces of nature for purposes of destruction may have to bear the responsibility of opening the door to an era of devastation on an unimaginable scale." Determined to do what he could to stop the momentum toward using the bomb, Szilard asked his friend Einstein to give him a letter of introduction to President Roosevelt. But just as the meeting was being arranged, an announcement came over the radio that Roosevelt was dead.

Would Einstein's great prestige have swayed the decision? It is doubtful. Einstein, known to be sympathetic to socialism and pacifism, was excluded from the Manhattan Project and did not know about the momentous decisions being made to drop the bombs on Hiroshima and Nagasaki.

One adviser to Harry Truman took a strong position against the atomic bombing of Japan: Undersecretary of the Navy Ralph Bard. As a member of Stimson's Interim Committee, at first he agreed with the decision to use the bomb on a Japanese city, but then changed his mind. He wrote a memorandum to the committee talking about the reputation of the United States "as a great humanitarian nation" and suggesting the Japanese be warned and that some assurance about the treatment of the emperor might induce the Japanese to surrender. It had no effect.

A few military men of high rank also opposed the decision. General Dwight Eisenhower, fresh from leading the Allied armies to victory in Europe, met with Stimson just after the successful test of the bomb in Los Alamos. He told Stimson he opposed use of the bomb because the Japanese were ready to surrender. Eisenhower later recalled, "I hated to see our country be the first to use such a weapon." General Hap Arnold, head of the army air force, believed Japan could be brought to surrender without the bomb. The fact that important military leaders saw no need for the bomb lends weight to the idea that the reasons for bombing Hiroshima and Nagasaki were political.

In the operations of U.S. foreign policy after World War II, there were a few bold people who rejected Machiavellian subservience and refused to accept the going orthodoxies. Senator William Fulbright of Arkansas was at the crucial meeting of advisers when President Kennedy was deciding whether to proceed with plans to invade Cuba. Arthur Schlesinger, who was there, wrote later that "Fulbright, speaking in an emphatic and incredulous way, denounced the whole idea."

During the Vietnam War, advisers from MIT and Harvard were among the fiercest advocates of ruthless bombing , but a few rebelled. One of the earliest was James Thomson, a Far East expert in the State Department who resigned his post and wrote an eloquent article in the *Atlantic Monthly* criticizing the U.S. presence in Vietnam.

While Henry Kissinger was playing Machiavelli to Nixon's prince, at least three of his aides objected to his support for an invasion of Cambodia in 1970. William Watts, asked to coordinate the White House announcement on the invasion of Cambodia, declined and wrote a letter of resignation. He was confronted by Kissinger aide General Al Haig, who told him, "You have an order from your Commander in Chief." He, therefore, could not resign, Haig said, Watts replied, "Oh yes I can—and I have!" Roger Morris and Anthony Lake, asked to write the speech for President Nixon justifying the invasion, refused and instead wrote a joint letter of resignation.

The most dramatic action of dissent during the war in Vietnam came from Daniel Ellsberg, a Ph.D. in economics from Harvard who had served in the Marines and held important posts in the Department of Defense, the Department of State, and the embassy in Saigon. He had been a special assistant to Henry Kissinger and then worked for the Rand Corporation a private "think tank" of brainy people who contracted to do top-secret research for the U.S. government. When the Rand

Corporation was asked to assemble a history of the Vietnam War, based on secret documents, Ellsberg was appointed as one of the leaders of the project. But he had already begun to feel pangs of conscience about the brutality of the war being waged by his government. He had been out in the field with the military, and what he saw persuaded him that the United States did not belong in Vietnam. Then, reading the documents and helping to put together the history, he saw how many lies had been told to the public and was reinforced in his feelings.

With the help of a former Rand employee he had met in Vietnam, Anthony Russo, Ellsberg secretly photocopied the entire 7,000-page history—the "Pentagon Papers" as they came to be called—and distributed them to certain members of Congress as well as to *The New York Times*. When the *Times*, in a journalistic sensation, began printing this "top-secret" document, Ellsberg was arrested and put on trial. The counts against him could have brought a prison sentence of 130 years. But while the jury deliberated the judge learned, through the Watergate scandal, that Nixon's "plumbers" had tried to break into Ellsberg's psychiatrist's office to find damaging material and he declared the case tainted and called off the trial.

Ellsberg's was only one of a series of resignations from government that took place during and after the Vietnam War. A number of operatives of the CIA quit their jobs in the late sixties and early seventies and began to write and speak about the secret activities of the agency—for example, Victor Marchetti, Philip Agee, John Stockwell, Frank Snepp, and Ralph McGehee.

For the United States, as for others countries, Machiavellianism dominates foreign policy, but the courage of a small number of dissenters suggests the possibility that some day the larger public will no longer accept that kind of "realism." Machiavelli himself might have smiled imperiously at this suggestion, and said, "You're wasting your time. Nothing will change. It's human nature."

That claim is worth exploring.

20

Aggressive Liberalism

For me, as for many others, the Vietnam war became an occasion for examining larger questions about the historical role of the United States in the world, particularly its record of expansion, both on the continent and overseas. As part of such an examination I wrote this essay, which appeared in *The Politics of History* (Beacon Press, 1970; Illinois University Press, 1990).

The concept of paradox is useful to our innocence. We keep it as a last defense, first erecting two other barriers. The first is not to look for, or not to see, those facts that challenge our deepest beliefs. The second is (when the world will not tolerate our ignorance) to keep separate in our consciousness those elements which, brought together, would explode the myths of our culture. When both those restraining walls collapse, we fall back, as an emergency measure, on the explanation: It's one of those paradoxes—an incredible but true combination.

With this triple defense, the liberal democracy of the Western world, bedecked with universal suffrage, parliamentary representation, technological progresss, mass education, Bills of Rights, social welfare, has managed to maintain its reputation for beneficence—despite its record of imperialism, war, racism, and exploitation. The unpleasant facts are first ignored (or made pallid by judicious juxtaposition with the more blatant sins of others). Then they are kept in a different compartment of the brain. Then, when the brain is so jostled that separation becomes impossible, the essential goodness of what we call Western Civilization is kept intact by the concept of paradox. Thus, liberalism can remain unscratched by the most prurient of juxtapositions, and the entire social system for which it is the shorthand symbol—the bad as well as the good—can remain unquestioned.

It is the first line of defense that this essay will deal with—the forgetting of discomfiting facts. The myth that refuses to be discomfited is that the United States, as might be expected from its behavior at home, is a peculiarly decent nation abroad.

Perhaps we took the myth, along with mother's milk, from British liberalism. A British historian, Geoffrey Barraclough, writing of German expansionism at the time of the First World War, says: "Easy though it is to criticize the imperialism of the French and British in Africa or China, their worst enormities simply do not compare. For all its faults, British imperialism had a genuine idealistic component, a sense of service and mission expressed in India by Curzon and in Egypt by Cromer."

"Idealistic components" have always been handy in aggressive international behavior. The chastity of Helen in the Trojan Wars, the sanctity of Christ's birthplace in the Crusades—and one can multiply the components indefinitely—no more altered the basic fact of conquest, murder, exploitation than did the more sophisticated rationale of the British liberals in the Boer War. As D.A.N. Jones has written about Winston Churchill's role at the time:

> Churchill lent an air of nobility to ugly realities. He had come to Parliament in 1901 as the war correspondent from South Africa, able to present the Boer War as a grand duel between blood-brothers. Some, he said, in his maiden speech, were prepared to "stigmatize this as a war of greed... This war from beginning to end has only been a war of duty."

Churchill praised the white enemy for not arming the black population: "The Black Peril...is the one bond of union between the European races." In a letter to his wife in 1907, Churchill, a junior Minister in the Liberal Government, talks of "...150,000 more natives under our direct control.... There will not, I think, be any bloodshed.... Thus the Empire grows under Radical Administration!"

Was this a "paradox" of British liberalism? Only if one ignores parallel features of liberalism at home which cast doubt on the total appraisal traditionally made of liberal democracy in the West. For instance, Churchill is "all for government intervention to assist the poor, to take the trailways and canals into public ownership, to establish a national minimum wage. It was all talk." He was also saying: "As for tramps and wastrels, there ought to be proper Labour Colonies where they could be... made to realise their duty to the State." And in 1911, as Home Secretary, he accompanied the police who were after some foreign-born burglars alleged to be anarchists. The suspects' house was burned down; two corpses were found, and Churchill wrote to the Prime Minister.

> I thought it better to let the house burn down rather than spend good British lives in rescuing those ferocious rascals. I think I shall have to stiffen the administration of the Aliens Act a little....

To reply to the claim of "paradox" in American liberalism, we would have to place its external conduct alongside the facts of its domestic policies. But first, the external conduct itself requires a more scrupulous examination than is usually given: whether in the elementary school textbooks which glorify America's wars, or in the more sophisticated academic circles where benign motives and other "idealistic components" are thought to make American foreign policy notably more admirable than that of other nations.*

---

* This insistence on our purity reaches absurd lengths. In 1968, *Life* magazine carried a picture of a Vietnamese girl whose leg was amputated after she was shot down by a United States helicopter. Dr. Howard Rusk, President of the World Rehabilitation Fund, wrote: "I think the readers of *Life* should know that young Tran would not have had an artificial limb had it not been for the American people working through the U.S. Agency for International Development."

A quick survey of American foreign policy shows that aggressiveness, violence, and deception accompanied, from our first years as a nation, the development of those domestic attributes which (seen in isolation from other domestic traits) made us the prototype of Western liberal democracy. This survey is of course a selective one, but for purposes of taking a hard look at our nation in a time of social crisis, it is a useful corrective to more orthodox selection. I suspect there is an important difference between individuals and nations which supports the idea of a critical selection. For a person, the overlooking of past miscreancy may have a positive effect on future conduct, as a psychological spur to change. For nations, there is not that sensitivity. A hardened, mindless mechanism requires not psychological encouragement but a taking apart and reassembling by its citizens—a task so arduous as to be spurred only by a sense of great peril, reinforced by a concentrated recollection of the number of times the mechanism has failed.

It was in our first diplomatic efforts as a new nation—the making of the peace treaty with England—that, despite the nobility of sentiment that accompanied a war for independence and the goals of the Declaration of Independence, we began to show the cupidity of our elders. Bradford Perkins, in his review of Richard B. Morris' *The Peacemakers*, makes the point as precisely as one could make it:

> ...like most American historians, Richard Morris seems to assume that, because the envoys served a noble people, their cynical and even dishonest efforts are to be excused, whereas their European counterparts are to be condemned because they served less enlightened states. In fact Jay, Franklin, and Adams triumphed precisely because they adopted the brutal morality of their contemporaries. They betrayed their instructions and the spirit of the alliance with France to obtain great benefits for their country. They cannot, as Morris seems to imply, be defended on moral grounds. They initiated, their contemporaries echoed, and their countrymen since have reaffirmed the false claim that Americans normally act with a morality superior to that of statesmen of other nations.

The peace that followed the Revolutionary War was a nervous one, accompanied by the first waves of post-independence nationalist passion. The British were holding on to their military and trading posts on the northern frontier, the Spanish were in the Floridas to the south, the French soon in possession of New Orleans and the vast Louisiana territory to the north, and the Indians everywhere. War fever rose and fell in those years, against the British under Washington, against the French under Adams (intensified by the French Revolution), against also (ironically—but irony is normal in international affairs) those Irish revolutionaries who came to this country with the same fierce anti-British feeling that we held in our Revolution.

From the first, aggressive expansion was a constant of national ideology and policy, whether the administration was "liberal" or "conservative"—that is, Federalist or Republican, Whig or Democrat, Democrat or Republican. The first and greatest act of territorial expansion was taken by Jefferson, in a legally dubious purchase, the President conveniently overlooking the fact that he was receiving, in effect, stolen goods (for Napoleon was violating a treaty with Spain by selling Louisiana).

Expansionism was given a moral justification; the nation had a "natural right" to security in the West, it was said. This was the customary jump in modern history, from an idealistic nationalism invoked to justify independence from colonial rule, to the stretching out over others' territory by a new nation. "The very peoples who had drunk most deeply of the new humanitarian nationalism succumbed most rapidly to the expansionist intoxication which led into the age of imperialism," writes Arthur K. Weinberg, in his classic study, *Manifest Destiny*.

France had leaped from Rousseau to Napoleon, and the United States from the Declaration of Independence to (as Weinberg puts it) "the extension of its rule over an alien people—Indians—without their consent." And it was the author of the phrase "consent of the governed," Jefferson himself, who sent troops into the Louisiana Territory to guard against Indian outbreaks at the time of purchase. He had written in 1787 that "it may be taken for a certainty that not a foot of land will ever be taken from the Indians without their own consent." The argument now used to justify taking this land from the Indians was that they were not cultivating it. But a score of years later, when the Indians began to settle down in the South and to cultivate the land, they were driven out (by Andrew Jackson, Jefferson's descendant in the "liberal" tradition).*

Expansionism, with its accompanying excuses, seems to be a constant characteristic of the nation-state, whether liberal or conservative, social-ist or capitalist. I am not trying to argue that the liberal-democratic state is especially culpable, only that it is not less so than other nations. Russian expansionism into Eastern Europe, the Chinese moving into Tibet and battling with India over border territories—seem as belligerent as the pushings of that earlier revolutionary upstart, the United States. And in these cases, the initial revolution followed by others, led to a para-noid fear of revolution beyond the real potential.

Thus, six years after the American Revolution, France was convulsed in hers. After the turn of the century, Latin America caught fire: Haiti the first, suspiciously close to the American shore, then Venezuela, Argentina, Chile, and the rest. Europe's despots pointed accusingly at the United States, much as we now point to Soviet Russia (or more lately to China or Cuba) whenever there are rumblings of change anywhere in the world. The philosophy of Manifest Destiny in America was not far from the Soviet rationale today, that (in Weinberg's words) "one nation has a preeminent social worth, a distinctively lofty mission, and consequently unique rights in the application of moral principles." Socialism and lib-eralism both have advantages over feudal monarchies in their ability to throw a benign light over vicious actions.

On the eve of the war of 1812, the Madison administration, by a combination of subversive agitation and deception, took from under the nose of Spain the territory of West Florida, a strip of land along the Gulf of Mexico reaching as far west as Baton Rouge. Expansionist elements in

---

* For an account of the long, murderous battle against the Indians see John Tebbel and Keith Jennison, *The American Indian Wars*, Harper & Row, 1960.

the Southern states, encouraged and perhaps helped materially by the Madison administration, revolted against Spanish authority, set up a Lone Star Republic, and asked to join the United States. It was a preview in certain respects of the later annexation of Texas. According to Thomas A. Bailey, Secretary of State James Monroe "went so far as to falsify the dates of certain important documents" to show that the territory belonged to the United States as part of the Louisiana Purchase. Spain was too heavily involved in war with Napoleon to do much about it, but several years later, the *London Times* said: "Mr. Madison's dirty, swindling manoeuvres in respect to Louisiana and the Floridas remain to be punished."

A century and a half of historical research have not solved the question of exactly why the United States went to war with England in 1812. The grievance concerning British impressment of American seamen seems hopelessly knotted with expansionist aims. But, whatever the complex of actual reasons, there is no doubt about the powerful generation of expansionist sentiment at this point in American history. Congressman John Randolph of Virginia, suspicious of the imperial designs of John Calhoun and Henry Clay, told the House of Representatives that the impressment issue was false. "Agrarian cupidity, not maritime right, urges the war," he said. "Ever since the report of the Committee...we have heard but one word—like a whip-poor-will, but one eternal monotonous tone—Canada! Canada! Canada!"

As if to corroborate this accusation, the *Nashville Clarion* asked: "Where is it written in the book of fate that the American Republic shall not stretch her limits from the Capes of the Chesapeake to Nootka Sound, from the isthmus of Panama to Hudson Bay?" The entire North American continent lay waiting.

The war of 1812 ended too indecisively for the United States to extend her territorial possessions at the expense of Britain. But there was Spain, controlling Florida. In 1817, Andrew Jackson went into action. Given the right by the American Government to cross the Florida border in pursuit of pillagers—Seminole Indians, runaway slaves, white renegades—he did just that, and then more. He seized most of the important

Florida posts, confiscated the royal Spanish archives, replaced the Spanish governor with an American, executed two Englishmen, and declared that United States tax laws would operate in Florida. For this, he became a national hero.

This led to what appears benignly in our textbook charts as "The Florida Purchase." Secretary of State John Quincy Adams insisted that Spain cede Florida, and promised to take care of American citizens' claims against Spain, amounting to five million dollars, but not a cent went to Spain for the Florida territory. As Bailey sums up:

> However much we may applaud the masterly diplomacy of Adams, there are features of the negotiation that are not altogether savory. Spain, to be sure, was shuffling, dilatory, and irresponsible; the United States was rough, highhanded and arrogant. Some writers have called the acquisition of Florida a case of international bullying. Others have called it Manifest Destiny—the falling of ripe fruit.

The Monroe Doctrine has been vested with a good deal of patriotic sentiment, accompanied by only a vague sense of what it was all about. In the 1920s, Christian Science leader Mary Baker Eddy took a full-page ad in *The New York Times*, heading it: "I believe strictly in the Monroe Doctrine, in our Constitution, and in the laws of God."

As we look into it, the Monroe Doctrine begins to look like the common tendency of all new nations to build a *cordon sanitaire* around themselves, and indeed to stretch that far beyond the needs of self-defense. Russia in Eastern Europe, China in South Asia, Egypt in the Middle East, have all showed the same behavior. And in August of 1960, the prime Minister of Ghana, Kwame Nkrumah, told his National Assembly that he "would not be so presumptuous as to put forward a Monroe Doctrine for Africa" but that he thought African problems should be settled by African states. His statement had just the tone of righteousness and just the tone of paternal supervision that marked the United States in 1823, when James Monroe's presidential message to Congress promised that the United States would not interfere in the internal concerns of European countries, but also warned that "we should consider any attempt on their part to extend their system to any portion of this hemisphere as dangerous to our peace and safety."

There is considerable doubt that the Monroe Doctrine saved either independence or democracy in Latin America, but there is little doubt that it served as a justification, by President Polk and later by Theodore Roosevelt, for the expansion of American influence in Latin America. Interestingly, Metternich in central Europe saw this commonplace action of modern nationalism with the same ideological phobia that the United States sees the Soviet Union and other Communist nations. He responded to the Monroe Doctrine as follows: "These United States of America..lend new strength to the apostles of sedition and reanimate the courage of every conspirator. If this flood of evil doctrines and pernicious examples should extend over the whole of America, what would become of our religious and political institutions..."

The spirit of Manifest Destiny was strong in those very decades of the early nineteenth century when the nation was creating institutions marking it as liberal and democratic: the extension of suffrage, the popular election of the President, the spread of public education, the flowering of literature. One of the nation's leading orators, Edward Everett, in an oration commemorating the battle of Bunker Hill in 1836, told his audience:

> ...wherever there are men living, laboring, suffering, enjoying—there are our brothers. Look then still further abroad, honored friends and patriots! Behold in distant countries, in other quarters of the globe, the influence of your example and achievements in stimulating the progress of social improvement. Behold the mighty spirit of Reform striding like a giant through the civilized world and trampling down established abuses at every step!... Behold him working out his miracles in France, knocking off the shackles of neighboring nations in Spanish America, pursuing his course, sometimes triumphant, sometimes temporarily trodden under foot, betrayed by false friends, overwhelmed by superior force, but still in the main, forward and onward over Spain, Portugal, Italy, Germany, Greece!

The liberal West, now fat, rich, and spread-eagled over the world, points with alarm at the upstart righteousness of the Communist states, the messianic fervor of the new nationalism in Asia and Africa. But liberalism, at a similar state in its development, showed the same character. Tocqueville wrote in the 1830s: "Nothing is more embarrassing in the ordinary intercourse of life, than this irritable patriotism of the Americans."

In the same period the most popular American historian was George Bancroft, who saw American democracy as God's special gift to the universe. His historical study of the United States, Bancroft said, aimed "to follow the steps by which a favoring Providence, calling our institutions into being, has conducted the nation to its present happiness and glory." Shall we rest on the explanation of "paradox" when we recall that at this same time, the nation was putting people in prison for debt, herding free men into labor gangs, under the most brutal conditions, and enslaving that one-sixth of its population which was black?

The administration of Andrew Jackson, who is seen sometimes as an early New Dealer, a conveyer of the liberal Jeffersonian tradition, was a particularly truculent one. The Cherokees were established in the South as a separate nation, by treaty after treaty which they signed with the United States. They were industrious, progressive, and peaceful. Their government was more democratic and their educational system more advanced than those of Georgia, North Carolina, and Tennessee, in whose mountain fastnesses the Cherokees maintained their society. When Georgia in 1832 defied a Supreme Court ruling that only the national government had jurisdiction over Cherokee territory, Andrew Jackson supported Georgia with his famous statement: "John Marshall has made his decision, now let him enforce it."

Jackson, after all, was an old Indian fighter, and he pushed through Congress an Indian Removal Act to force the Cherokees out. A few years later, General Winfield Scott invaded with 7000 troops. The Cherokees were put in concentration camps, their homes burned, and 14,000 of them herded onto the long trek westward, the "Trail of Tears," during which 4000 men, women and children died.

Any confidence in the special benignity of a "democratic" nation's foreign policy is shaken, at the least, by this episode. Four years after the crushing of the Hungarian revolt, Premier Khrushchev of the Soviet Union declared that the Hungarian situation was now settled to everyone's satisfaction. Andrew Jackson's handpicked successor, President Martin Van Buren, said about the Cherokee removal operation: "The measures authorized by Congress at its last session have had the happiest effects... The Cherokees have emigrated without any apparent reluctance."

It was an aggressive war against Mexico that extended the nation's boundaries to the Pacific. In the 1819 treaty with Spain the United States had given up any claim to Texas. But this did not stop it from trying to bribe Mexican officials to sell Texas, as by United States Minister Anthony Butler in Jackson's administration. This failing, it gave active support to the revolution which separated Texas from Mexico and made it, for ten years, the Lone Star State. The United States had its eye not only on Texas, but on California and all the land between-about half of what was then Mexico. After Texas was annexed in 1845, President Polk sent secret instructions to his confidential agent in California, Thomas O. Larkin, to work for annexation.

Polk first tried to buy California and New Mexico, but Mexico refused, whereupon he sent troops into the disputed territory between the Nueces River and the Rio Grande, which both Texas and Mexico claimed. When Polk took the question of war to his cabinet, the suggestion was made that it would be better for Mexico to start the war. By some remarkable coincidence, a dispatch that same night reported Mexicans coming into the disputed area, and a battle ensued, with sixteen American casualties. Polk asked Congress to declare war, saying that Mexico "has invaded territory and shed American blood upon the American soil." Polk's claim to be protecting Texas was rather weak, in view of the fact that in nine years Mexico had made no effort to retake Texas.

The war was won without difficulty, and the 1848 Treaty of

Guadalupe Hidalgo gave the United States what it wanted: New Mexico, California, and the disputed territory in Texas—altogether, half of Mexico. The States could even point to its restraint in not taking all of Mexico. During the war, that thought had been widespread. At a Jackson Day dinner, Senator Dickinson of New York had offered a toast to "a more perfect Union, embracing the whole of the North American continent." The liberal *New York Evening Post* urged America not to withdraw from Mexico, saying:

> Now we ask, whether any man can coolly contemplate the idea of recalling our troops from the territory we at present occupy and.. resign this beautiful country to the custody of the ignorant cowards and profligate ruffians who have ruled it for the last 25 years? Why, humanity cries out against it. Civilization and Christianity protest.

Expansionism was neither liberal nor conservative, Southern or Northern. It was a trait of the American nation, as of other nations, as of any unit bursting with power and privilege in a competitive, lawless world. The sentiment of the *New York Post* was not much different from that of Jefferson Davis, the Senator from Mississippi, who wrote just before the Civil War:

> We may expand so as to include the whole world. Mexico, Central America, South America, Cuba, the West India Islands, and even England and France we might annex without inconvenience...allowing them with their local legislatures to regulate their local affairs in their own way. And this sir, is the mission of this Republic and its ultimate destiny.

It was, indeed, in the direction of worldwide power, that the United States Government moved. It expanded, in the years between the Revolution and the Civil War, from a thin strip along the Atlantic to a huge continental power fronting the oceans. It did this by purchase and by pressure, by aggression, by deceit, and by war. It used these varied weapons against Spaniards, Frenchmen, Indians, Mexicans—and all with an air of arrogant righteousness, with the idea that to spread the American flag far and wide was to confer on other peoples the greatest gift in the world.

After 1890, we moved out into the Caribbean and the Pacific, as far as the coastal waters of China. That story is too well known to recount in detail: the "splendid little war" with Spain; the annexation of Hawaii, and the Philippines and the ugly war of extermination against the Filipino rebels; the taking of Puerto Rico and the establishment of a protectorate over Cuba; the shrewd creation of a Republic of Panama, pulling the site for a canal from under Colombia; the waves of marines into the Caribbean—Haiti, the Dominican Republic, Nicaragua; the bombardment and occupation of Vera Cruz; in the meantime the concern with profit and influence in China and Japan by the judicious use of gunboats, dollars, and diplomacy. With World War I we became a banker of the world; with World War II we spread military bases onto every land mass, every ocean in the world, intervened openly or stealthily in Greece, Lebanon, Guatemala, Cuba, the Dominican Republic, Korea, Vietnam. By 1969, the Japanese had to protest the use of their former island, Okinawa, to store deadly nerve gas for American military use.

These, in terse summary, are the facts we tend either to ignore or to so mix into the rich potpourri of American history as to obscure them. Extricated, they force us to deal with them alongside the kindly view of our society as a summit of liberal, democratic achievement in world history. Refusing to simply separate "liberalism" at home from aggression abroad, refusing also to end the discussion by speaking of "paradox," we can attempt a reconciliation from one or another direction.

That is, we can find that our behavior abroad is not as bad as it seems on first look, that it is indeed invested with some of the saving characteristics we find in domestic liberalism. For instance, Frederick Merk, in *Manifest Destiny and Mission in American History, a Reinterpretation*, is unhappy with the idea that manifest destiny and imperialism represent the actual American spirit. He finds they are exceptions, and that the true American mood was that of "mission," of liberating other peoples, that the United States has been, in the main, "idealistic, self-denying, hopeful of divine favor for national aspirations, though not sure of it."

I would suggest another way of looking at the facts: that there is a similar principle, operating in domestic affairs and foreign affairs—for presumably liberal states as for other kinds of states: that in a world which has not yet developed either the mind or the mechanism for humane cooperation, power and privilege tend to be as rapacious as the degree of resistance by the victims will permit. That aggression at home is more disguised, more sporadic, more controlled than aggression abroad, comes from the development of countervailing forces at home, while those abroad have usually been helpless before the marauding foreign power. Where internal groups have been similarly helpless they have been treated as ruthlessly as enemies in wartime: the blacks, the Indians, the workingmen before they organized, the students when they dared to challenge authority.

All this suggests that we need to stop looking with special fondness on that group of Western states which represent, in those millions of textbooks distributed in high schools and colleges "Western civilization." Their external behavior is not an unfortunate departure from character. It is what their internal behavior would be if undeterred by a population whose greater literacy and greater activity (a necessity of modern industrial development) enabled them to at least partially resist.

The idealist rhetoric surrounding the foreign policies of liberal states is only a variant on the historic use of rhetoric by aggressive civilizations in the past: the Greeks had their noble excuses for destroying the people of Melos: the Popes drove Christian armies forward with words of holy purity; the socialist states invent socialist excuses for their assaults. A bit of historical perspective may help us to deal, in our own time, with the missionary-soldiers of other nations and of ours.

21

Just and
Unjust War

I enlisted in the Army Air Corps in World War II and was an eager bombardier, determined to do everything I could to help defeat fascism. Yet, at the end of the war, when I collected my little mementos—my photos, logs of some of my missions—I wrote on the folder, without really thinking, and surprising myself: "Never Again." In the years after the war, I began to plumb the reasons for that spontaneous reaction, and came to the conclusions which I describe in the following essay, published as a chapter in my book *Declarations of Independence* (HarperCollins, 1990).

Years before (in *Postwar America,* Bobbs Merrill, 1973), I had written an essay called "The Best of Wars," in which I questioned—I was unaware of anyone else asking the same question—the total acceptance of World War II. After my own experience in that war, I had moved away from my own rather orthodox view that there are just wars and unjust wars, to a universal rejection of war as a solution to any human problem. Of all the positions I have taken over the years on questions of history and politics, this has undoubtedly aroused the most controversy. It is obviously a difficult viewpoint to present persuasively. I try to do that here, and leave it to the reader to judge whether I have succeeded.

There are some people who do not question war. In 1972, the general who was head of the U.S. Strategic Air Command told an interviewer, "I've been asked often about my moral scruples if I had to send the planes out with hydrogen bombs. My answer is always the same. I would be concerned only with my professional responsibility."

It was a Machiavellian reply. Machiavelli did not ask if making war was right or wrong. He just wrote about the best way to wage it so as to conquer the enemy. One of his books is called *The Art of War*.

That title might make artists uneasy. Indeed, artists—poets, novelists, and playwrights as well as musicians, painters, and actors—have shown a special aversion to war. Perhaps because, as the playwright Arthur Miller once said, "When the guns boom, the arts die." But that would make their interest too self-centered; they have always been sensitive to the fate of the larger society round them. They have questioned war, whether in the fifth century before Christ, with the plays of Euripedes, or in modern times, with the paintings of Goya and Picasso.

Machiavelli was being *realistic*. Wars were going to be fought. The only question was how to win them.

Some people have believed that war is not just inevitable but desirable. It is adventure and excitement, it brings out the best qualities in men—courage, comradeship, and sacrifice. It gives respect and glory to a country. In 1897, Theodore Roosevelt wrote to a friend, "In strict confidence...I should welcome almost any war, for I think this country needs one."

In our time, fascist regimes have glorified war as heroic and ennobling. Bombing Ethiopia in 1935, Mussolini's son-in-law Count Ciano described the explosions as an aesthetic thrill, as having the beauty of a flower unfolding.

In the 1980s, two writers of a book on war see it as an effective instrument of national policy and say that even nuclear war can, under certain circumstances, be justified. They are contemptuous of "the pacifist passions: self-indulgence and fear," and of "American statesmen, who believe victory is an archaic concept." They say, "The bottom line in war and hence in political warfare is who gets buried and who gets to walk in the sun."

Most people are not that enamored of war. They see it as bad, but also as a possible means to something good. And so they distinguish between wars that are just and those that are unjust. The religions of the West and Middle East—Judaism, Christianity, and Islam—approve of violence and war under certain circumstances. The Catholic church has a specific doctrine of "just" and "unjust" war, worked out in some detail. Political philosophers today argue about which wars, or which actions in wars, may be considered just or unjust.

Beyond both viewpoints—the glorification of war and the weighing of good and bad wars—there is a third: that war is too evil to ever be just. The monk Erasmus, writing in the early sixteenth century, was repelled by war of any kind. One of his pupils was killed in battle and he reacted with anguish:

> Tell me, what had you to do with Mars, the stupidest of all the poet's gods, you who were consecrated to the Muses, nay to Christ? Your youth, your beauty, your gentle nature, your honest mind—what had they to do with the flourishing of trumpets, the bombards, the swords?

Erasmus described war: "There is nothing more wicked, more disastrous, more widely destructive, more deeply tenacious, more loathsome." He said this was repugnant to nature: "Whoever heard of a hundred thousand animals rushing together to butcher each other, as men do everywhere?"

Erasmus saw war as useful to governments, for it enabled them to enhance their power over their subjects: "...once war has been declared, then all the affairs of the State are at the mercy of the appetites of a few."

This absolute aversion to war of any kind is outside the orthodoxy of modern thinking. In a series of lectures at Oxford University in the 1970s, English scholar Michael Howard talked disparagingly about

Erasmus. He called him simplistic, unsophisticated, and someone who did not see beyond the "surface manifestations" of war. He said,

> With all [Erasmus's] genius he was not a profound political analyst, nor did he ever have to exercise the responsibilities of power. Rather he was the first in that long line of humanitarian thinkers for whom it was enough to chronicle the horrors of war in order to condemn it.

Howard had praise for Thomas More: "Very different was the approach of Erasmus's friend, Thomas More; a man who had exercised political responsibility and, perhaps in consequence, saw the problem in all its complexity." More was a realist; Howard says,

> He accepted, as thinkers for the next two hundred years were to accept, that European society was organized in a system of states in which war was an inescapable process for the settlement of differences in the absence of any higher common jurisdiction. That being the case, it was a requirement of humanity, of religion and of common sense alike that those wars should be fought in such a manner as to cause as little damage as possible. For better or worse war was an institution which could not be eliminated from the international system. All that could be done about it was, so far as possible, to codify its rationale and to civilize its means.

Thus, Machiavelli said: Don't question the ends of the prince, just tell him how best to do what he wants to do, make the means more *efficient*. Thomas More said: You can't do anything about the ends, but try to make the means more *moral*.

In the 400 years following the era of Machiavelli and More, making war more humane became the preoccupation of certain liberal "realists." Hugo Grotius, writing a century after More, proposed laws to govern the waging of war (*Concerning the Law of War and Peace*). The beginning of the twentieth century saw international conferences at The Hague in the Netherlands and at Geneva in Switzerland which drew up agreements on how to wage war.

These realistic approaches however, had little effect on the reality of war. Rather than becoming more controlled, war became more uncontrolled and more deadly, using more horrible means and killing more noncombatants than ever before in the history of mankind. We note the use of poison gas in World War I, the bombardment of cities in World War II, the atomic destruction of Hiroshima and Nagasaki near the end of that war, the use of napalm in Vietnam, and the chemical warfare in the Iran-Iraq war of the early 1980s.

Albert Einstein, observing the effects of attempts to "humanize" wars, became more and more anguished. In 1932, he attended a conference of sixty nations in Geneva and listened to the lengthy discussions of which weapons were acceptable and which were not, which forms of killing were legitimate and which were not.

Einstein was a shy, private person, but he did something extraordinary for him: he called a press conference in Geneva. The international press turned out in force to hear Einstein, already world famous for his theories of relativity. Einstein told the assembled reporters, "One does not make wars less likely by formulating rules of warfare....War cannot be humanized. It can only be abolished." But the Geneva conference went on, working out rules for "humane" warfare, rules that were repeatedly ignored in the world war soon to come, a war of endless atrocities.

In early 1990, President George Bush, while approving new weapons systems for nuclear warheads (of which the United States had about 30,000) and refusing to join the Soviet Union in stopping nuclear testing, was willing to agree to destroy chemical weapons, but only over a ten-year period. Such are the absurdities of "humanizing" war.

Liberal States and Just Wars: Athens

The argument that there are just wars often rests on the social system of the nation engaging in war. It is supposed that if a "liberal" state is at war with a "totalitarian" state, then the war is justified. The beneficent nature of a government is assumed to give rightness to the wars it wages.

Ancient Athens has been one of the most admired of all societies, praised for its democratic institutions and its magnificent cultural achievements. It had enlightened statesmen (Solon and Pericles), pioneer historians (Herodotus and Thucydides), great philosophers (Plato and Aristotle), and an extraordinary quartet of playwrights (Aeschylus, Sophocles, Euripides, and Aristphanes). When it went to war in 431 BC against its rival power, the city-state of Sparta, the war seemed to be between a democratic society and a military dictatorship.

The great qualities of Athens were described early in that war by the Athenian leader Pericles at a public celebration for the warriors, dead or alive. The bones of the dead were placed in chests; there was an empty litter for the missing. There was a procession, a burial, and then Pericles spoke. Thucydides recorded Pericles' speech in his *History of the Peloponnesian War:*

> Before I praise the dead, I should like to point out by what principles of action we rose to power, and under what institutions and through what manner of life our empire became great. Our form of government does not enter into rivalry with the institutions of others.... It is true that we are called a democracy, for the administration is in the hands of the many and not of the few.... The law secures equal justice to all alike.... Neither is poverty a bar.... There is no exclusiveness in our public life.... At home the style of our life is refined.... Because of the greatness of our city the fruits of the whole earth flow in upon us.... And although our opponents are fighting for their homes and we on foreign soil, we seldom have any difficulty in overcoming them.... I have dwelt upon the greatness of Athens because I want to show you that we are contending for a higher prize than those who enjoy none of these privileges.

Similarly, American presidents in time of war have pointed to the qualities of the American system as evidence for the justness of the cause. Woodrow Wilson and Franklin Roosevelt were liberals, which gave credence to their words exalting the two world wars, just as the liberalism of Truman made going into Korea more acceptable and the idealism of Kennedy's New Frontier and Johnson's Great Society gave an early glow of righteousness to the war in Vietnam.

But we should take a closer look at the claim that liberalism at home carries over into military actions abroad.

The tendency, especially in time of war, is to exaggerate the difference between oneself and the opponent, to assume the conflict is between total good and total evil. It was true that Athens had certain features of political democracy. Each of ten tribes selected 50 representatives, by lot, to make a governing council of 500. Trial juries were large, from 100 to 1,000 people, with no judge and no professional lawyers; the cases were handled by the people involved.

Yet, these democratic institutions only applied to a minority of the population. A majority of the people—125,000 out off 225,000— were slaves. Even among the free people, only males were considered citizens with the right to participate in the political process.

Of the slaves, 50,000 worked in industry (this is as if, in the United States in 1990, 50 million people worked in industry as slaves) and 10,000 worked in the mines. H.D. Kitto, a leading scholar on Greek civilization and a great admirer of Athens, wrote: "The treatment of the miners was callous in the extreme, the only serious blot on the general humanity of the Athenians.. Slaves were often worked until they died." (To Kitto and others, slavery was only a "blot" on an otherwise wonderful society.)

The jury system in Athens was certainly preferable to summary executions by tyrants. Nevertheless, it put Socrates to death for speaking his mind to young people.

Athens was more democratic than Sparta, but this did not affect its addiction to warfare, to expansion into other territories, to the ruthless conduct of war against helpless peoples. In modern times we have seen the ease with which parliamentary democracies and constitutional republics have been among the most ferocious of imperialists. We recall the British and French empires of the nineteenth century and the United States as a world imperial power in this century.

Throughout the long war with Sparta, Athens' democratic institutions and artistic achievements continued. But the death toll was enormous. Pericles, on the eve of war, refused to make concessions that might have prevented it. In the second year of war, with the casualties mounting quickly, Pericles urged his fellow citizens not to weaken: "You have a great polis, and a great reputation; you must be worthy of them. Half the world is yours—the sea. For you the alternative to empire is slavery."

Pericles' kind of argument ("Ours is a great nation. It is worth dying for.") has persisted and been admired down to the present. Kitto, commenting on that speech by Pericles, again overcome by admiration, wrote,

> When we reflect that this plague was as awful as the Plague of London, and that the Athenians had the additional horror of being cooped up inside their fortifications by the enemy without, we must admire the greatness of the man who could talk to his fellow citizens like this, and the greatness of the people who could not only listen to such a speech at such a time but actually be substantially persuaded by it.

They were enough persuaded by it so that the war with Sparta lasted twenty-seven years. Athens lost through plague and war (according to Kitto's own estimate) perhaps one-fourth of its population.

However liberal it was for its free male citizens at home, Athens became more and more cruel to its victims in war, not just to its enemy Sparta, but to every one caught in the crossfire of the two antagonists. As the war went on, Kitto himself says, "a certain irresponsibility grew."

Could the treatment of the inhabitants of the island of Melos be best described as "a certain irresponsibility"? Athens demanded that the Melians submit to its rule. The Melians, however, argued (as reported by Thucydides), "It may be to your interest to be our masters, but how can it be ours to be your slaves?" The Melians would not submit. They fought and were defeated. Thucydides wrote, "The Athenians thereupon put to death all who were of military age, and made slaves of the women and children." (It was shortly after this event that Euripides wrote his great antiwar play, *The Trojan Women*).

What the experience of Athens suggests is that a nation may be relatively liberal at home and yet totally ruthless abroad. Indeed, it may more easily enlist its population in cruelty to others by pointing to the advantages at home. An entire nation is made into mercenaries, being paid with a bit of democracy at home for participating in the destruction of life abroad.

Liberalism at War

Liberalism at home, however, seems to become corrupted by war waged abroad. French philosopher Jean Jacques Rousseau noted that conquering nations "make war at least as much on their subjects as on their enemies." Tom Paine, in America, saw war as the creature of governments, serving their own interests, not the interests of justice for their citizens. "Man is not the enemy of man but through the medium of a false system of government." In our time, George Orwell has written that wars are mainly "internal."

One certain effect of war is to diminish freedom of expression. Patriotism becomes the order of the day, and those who question the war are seen as traitors, to be silenced and imprisoned.

Mark Twain, observing the United States at the turn of the century, its wars in Cuba and the Philippines, described in *The Mysterious Stranger* the process by which wars that are at first seen as unnecessary by the mass of the people become converted into "just" wars:

> The loud little handful will shout for war. The pulpit will warily and cautiously protest at first.... The great mass of the nation will rub its sleepy eyes, and will try to make out why there should be a war, and they will say earnestly and indignantly: "It is unjust and dishonorable and there is no need for war."
>
> Then the few will shout even louder.... Before long you will see a curious thing: anti-war speakers will be stoned from the platform, and free speech will be strangled by hordes of furious men who still agree with the speakers but dare not admit it....
>
> Next, the statesmen will invent cheap lies...and each man will be glad of these lies and will study them because they soothe his conscience; and thus he will bye and bye convince himself that the war is just and he will thank God for a better sleep he enjoys by his self-deception.

Mark Twain died in 1910. In 1917, the United States entered the slaughterhouse of the European war, and the process of silencing dissent and converting a butchery into a just war took place as he had predicted.

President Woodrow Wilson tried to rouse the nation, using the language of a crusade. It was a war, he said, "to end all wars." but large numbers of Americans were reluctant to join. A million men were needed, yet in the first six weeks after the declaration of war only 73,000 volunteered. It seemed that men would have to be compelled to fight by fear of prison, so Congress enacted a draft law.

The Socialist Party at the time was a formidable influence in the country. It had perhaps 100,000 members, and more than a thousand Socialists had been elected to office in 340 towns and cities. Probably a million Americans read Socialist newspapers. There were fifty-five weekly Socialist newspapers in Oklahoma, Texas, Louisiana, and Arkansas alone; over a hundred Socialists were elected to office in Oklahoma. The Socialist party candidate for president, Eugene Debs, got 900,000 votes in 1912 (Wilson won with 6 million).

A year before the United States entered the European war, Helen Keller, blind and deaf and a committed Socialist, told an audience at Carnegie Hall:

> Strike against war, for without you no battles can be fought! Strike against manufacturing shrapnel and gas bombs and all other tools of murder! Strike against preparedness that means death and misery to millions of human beings! Be not dumb, obedient slaves in an army of destruction! Be heroes in an army of construction!

The day after Congress declared war, the Socialist party met in an emergency convention and called the declaration "a crime against the American people." Antiwar meetings took place all over the country. In the local elections of 1917, Socialists made great gains. Ten Socialists were elected to the New York State legislature. In Chicago the Socialist party had won 3.6 percent of the vote in 1915 and it got 34.7 percent in 1917. But with the advent of war, speaking against it became a crime; Debs and hundreds of other Socialists were imprisoned.

When that war ended, 10 million men of various countries had died on the battlefields of Europe, and millions more had been blinded, maimed, gassed, shell-shocked, and driven mad. It was hard to find in that war any gain for the human race to justify that suffering, that death.

Indeed, when the war was studied years later, it was clear that no rational decision based on any moral principle had led the nations into war. Rather, there were imperial rivalries, greed for more territory, a lusting for national prestige, and the stupidity of revenge. And at the last moment, there was a reckless plunge by governments caught up in a series of threats and counterthreats, mobilizations and countermobilizations, ultimatums and counterultimatums, creating a momentum that mediocre leaders had neither the courage nor the will to stop. As described by Barbara Tuchman in her book *The Guns of August:*

> War pressed against every frontier. Suddenly dismayed, governments struggled and twisted to fend it off. It was no use. Agents at frontiers were reporting every cavalry patrol as a deployment to beat the mobilization gun. General staffs, goaded by their relentless timetables, were pounding the table for the signal to move lest their opponents gain an hour's head start. Appalled upon the brink, the chiefs of state who would be ultimately responsible for their country's fare attempted to back away, but the pull of military schedules dragged them forward.

Bitterness and disillusion followed the end of the war, and this was reflected in the literature of those years: Ernest Hemingway's *A Farewell to Arms*, John Dos Passo's *U.S.A.*, and Ford Madox Ford's *No More Parades*. In Europe, German war veteran Erich Maria Remarque wrote the bitter antiwar novel *All Quiet on the Western Front.*

In 1935 French playwright Jean Giradoux wrote *La guerre de Troi n'aura pas lieu (The Trojan War Will Not Take Place;* the English translation was retitled *Tiger at the Gates).* The war of the Greeks against Troy, more than a thousand years before Christ, was provoked, according to legend, by the kidnapping of the beautiful Helen by the Trojans. Giraudoux at one point uses Hecuba, an old woman, and Demokos, a Trojan soldier, to show how the ugliness of war is masked by attractive causes, as in this case, the recapture of Helen.

Demokos: Tell us before you go, Hecuba, what it is you think war looks like.

Hecuba: Like the bottom of a baboon. When the baboon is up in a tree, with its hind end facing us, there is the face of war exactly; scarlet, scaly, glazed, framed in a clotted filthy wig.

Demokos: So war has two faces: this you describe, and Helen's.

An Eager Bombardier

My own first impressions of something called war had come at the age of ten, when I read with excitement a series of books about "the boy allies"— A French boy, an English boy, an American boy, and a Russian boy, who became friends, united in the wonderful cause to defeat Germany in World War I. It was an adventure, a romance, told in a group of stories about comradeship and heroism. It was war cleansed of death and suffering.

If anything was left of that romantic view of war, it was totally extinguished when, at eighteen, I read a book by a Hollywood screenwriter named Dalton Trumbo (jailed in the 1950s for refusing to talk to the House Committee on Un-American Activities about his political affiliations). The book was called *Johnny Got His Gun*. It is perhaps, the most powerful antiwar novel ever written.

Here was war in its ultimate horror. A slab of flesh in an American uniform had been found on the battlefield, still alive, with no legs, no arms, no face, blind, deaf, unable to speak, but the heart still beating, the brain still functioning, able to think about his past, ponder his present condition, and wonder if he will ever be able to communicate with the world outside.

For him, the oratory of the politicians who sent him off to war—the language of freedom, democracy, and justice—is now seen as the ultimate hypocrisy. A mute, thinking torso on a hospital bed, he finds a way to communicate with a kindly nurse, and when a visiting delegation of military brass comes by to pin a medal on his body, he taps out a message. He says: Take me into the workplaces, into the schools, show me to the little children and to the college students, let them see what war is like.

Take me wherever there are parliaments and diets and congresses and chambers of statesmen. I want to be there when they talk about honor and justice and making the world safe for democracy and fourteen points and the self determination of peoples.... Put my glass case upon the speaker's desk and every time the gavel descends let me feel its vibration.... Then let them speak of trade policies and embargoes and new colonies and old grudges. Let them debate the menace of the yellow race and the white man's burden and the course of empire and why should we take all this crap off Germany or whoever the next Germany is.... Let them talk more munitions and airplanes and battleships and tanks and gases and why of course we've got to have them we can't get along without them how in the world could we protect the peace if we didn't have them....

But before they vote on them before they give the order for all the little guys to start killing each other let the main guy rap his gavel on my case and point down at me and say here gentlemen is the only issue before this house and that is are you for this thing here or are you against it.

Johnny Got His Gun had a shattering effect on me when I read it. It left me with a bone-deep hatred of war.

Around the same time I read a book by Walter Millis, *The Road to War*, which was an account of how the United States had been led into World War I by a series of lies and deceptions. Afterward I would learn more about those lies. For instance, the sinking of the ship *Lusitania* by German submarines was presented as a brutal, unprovoked act against a harmless passenger vessel. It was later revealed that the *Lusitania* was loaded with munitions, intended for use against Germany; the ship's manifest had been falsified to hide that. This didn't lessen the ugliness of the sinking, but did show something about the ways in which nations are lured into war.

Class consciousness accounted for some of my feeling about war. I agreed with the judgment of the Roman biographer Plutarch, who said, "The poor go to war, to fight and die for the delights, riches, and superfluities of others."

And yet, in early 1943, at the age of twenty-one, I enlisted in the U.S. Army Air Force. American troops were already in North Africa, Italy, and England; there was fierce fighting on the Russian front and the

United States and Britain were preparing for the invasion of Western Europe. Bombing raids were taking place daily on the continent, U.S. planes bombing during the day, British planes bombing at night. I was so anxious to get overseas and start dropping bombs that after my training in gunnery school and bombing school I traded places with another man who was scheduled to go overseas sooner than me.

I had learned to hate war. But this war was different. It was not for profit or empire, it was a people's war, a war against the unspeakable brutality of fascism. I had been reading about Italian fascism in a book about Mussolini by journalist George Seldes called *Sawdust Caesar*. I was inspired by his account of the Socialist Matteotti, who stood up in the Italian Chamber of Deputies to denounce the establishment of a dictatorship. The black-shirted thugs of Mussolini's party picked up Matteotti outside his home one morning and shot him to death. That was fascism.

Mussolini's Italy, deciding to restore the glory of the old Roman Empire, invaded the East African country of Ethiopia, a pitifully poor country. Its people, armed with spears and muskets, tried to fight off an Italian army equipped with the most modern weapons and with an air force that, unopposed, dropped bombs on the civilian populations of Ethiopian towns and villages. The Ethiopians who resisted were slaughtered, and finally surrendered.

American black poet Langston Hughes wrote,

The little fox is still—
The dogs of war have made their kill.

I was thirteen when this happened and was only vaguely aware of headlines: "Italian Planes Bomb Addis Ababa." But later I read about it and also about German Nazism. John Gunther's *Inside Europe* introduced me to the rise of Hitler, the SA, the SS, the attacks on the Jews, the shrill oratory of the little man with the mustache, and the monster rallies of Germans in sports stadia who shouted in unison: "Heil Hitler! Heil Hitler!" Opponents were beaten and murdered. I learned the phrase *concentration camp*.

I came across a book called *The Brown Book of the Nazi Terror*. It told in detail about the burning of the German Reichstag shortly after Hitler came to power and the arrest of Communists accused of setting the fire, clearly a frame-up. It told also of the extraordinary courage of the defendants, led by the remarkable Bulgarian Communist George Dimitrov, who rose in the courtroom to point an accusing finger at Hermann Goering, Hitler's lieutenant. Dimitrov tore the prosecution's case to shreds and denounced the Nazi regime. The defendants were acquitted by the court. It was an amazing moment, which would never be repeated under Hitler.

In 1936 Hitler and Mussolini sent their troops and planes to support the Spanish Fascist Franco, who had plunged his country into civil war to overthrow the mildly socialist Spanish government. The Spanish Civil War became the symbol all over the world of resistance to fascism, and young men—many of them socialists, Communists and anarchists—volunteered from a dozen countries, forming brigades (from the United States, the Abraham Lincoln Brigade), going immediately into battle against the better-equipped army of Franco. They fought heroically and died in great numbers. The Fascists won.

Then came the Hitler onslaught in Europe—Austria, Czechoslovakia, and Poland. France and England entered the war, and, a year after the quick defeat of France, three million German soldiers supported by tanks, artillery, and dive bombers turned eastward to attack the Soviet Union ("Operation Barbarossa") along a thousand-mile front.

Fascism had to be resisted and defeated. I had no doubts. This was a just war.

I was stationed at an airfield out in the countryside of East Anglia (between the towns of Diss and Eye), that part of England that bulges eastward toward the Continent. East Anglia was crowded with military airfields, from which hundreds of bombers went out every day across the Channel.

Our little airfield housed the 490th Bomb Group. Its job was to make sure that every morning twelve B17s—splendid-looking, low-winged, four-engined heavy bombers—each with a crew of nine, wearing sheepskin jackets and fur-lined boots over electrically heated suits and equipped with oxygen masks and throat mikes—were ready to fly. We would take off around dawn and assemble with other groups of twelve, and then these huge flotillas would make their way east. Our bomb bay was full; our fifty-caliber machine guns (four in the nose, one in the upper turret, one in the ball turret, two in the waist, and one in the tail) were loaded and ready for attacking fighter planes.

I remember one morning standing out on that airfield, arguing with another bombardier over who was scheduled to fly that morning's mission. The target was Regensburg, and Intelligence reported that it was heavily defended by antiaircraft guns, but the two of us argued heatedly over who was going to fly that mission. I wonder today, was his motive like mine—wanting to fly another mission to bring closer the defeat of fascism. Or was it because we had all been awakened at one AM in the cold dark of England in March, loaded onto trucks, taken to hours of briefings and breakfast, weighed down with equipment, and after going through all that, he did not want to be deprived of another step toward his air medal, another mission. Even though he might be killed.

Maybe that was partly my motive too, I can't be sure. But for me, it was also a war of high principle, and each bombing mission was a mission of high principle. The moral issue could hardly be clearer. The enemy could not be more obviously evil—openly espousing the superiority of the white Aryan, fanatically violent and murderous toward other nations, herding its own people into concentration camps, executing them if they dared dissent. The Nazis were pathological killers. They had to be stopped, and there seemed no other way but by force.

If there was such a thing as a just war, this was it. Even Dalton Trumbo, who had written *Johnny Got His Gun*, did not want his book to be reprinted, did not want that overpowering antiwar message to reach the American public, when a war had to be fought against fascism.

If, therefore, anyone wants to argue (as I am about to do) that there is no such thing as a just war, then World War II is the supreme test.

I flew the last bombing missions of the war, got my Air Medal and my battle stars. I was quietly proud of my participation in the great war to defeat fascism. But when I packed up my things at the end of the war and put my old navigation logs and snapshots and other mementos in a folder, I marked that folder, almost without thinking, "Never Again."

I'm still not sure why I did that, because it was not until years later that I began consciously to question the motives, the conduct, and the consequences of that crusade against fascism. The point was not that my abhorrence of fascism was in any way diminished. I still believed something had to be done to stop fascism. But that clear certainty of moral rightness that propelled me into the Air Force as an enthusiastic bombardier was now clouded over by many thoughts.

Perhaps my conversations with that gunner on the other crew, the one who loaned me *The Yogi and the Commisar*, gave me the first flickers of doubt. He spoke of the war as "an imperialist war," fought on both sides for national power. Britain and the United States opposed fascism only because it threatened their own control over resources and people. Yes, Hitler was a maniacal dictator and invader of other countries. But what of the British Empire and its long history of wars against native peoples to subdue them for the profit and glory of the empire? And the Soviet Union—was it not also a brutal dictatorship, concerned not with the working classes of the world but with its own national power?

I was puzzled. "Why," I asked my friend, "are you flying missions, risking your life, in a war you don't believe in?" His answer astonished me. "I'm here to speak to people like you."

I found out later he was a member of the Socialist Workers party; they opposed the war but believed that instead of evading military service they should enter it and propagandize against the war every moment they could. I couldn't understand this, but I was impressed by it. Two weeks after that conversation with him, he was killed on a mission over Germany.

After the war, my doubts grew. I was reading history. Had the United States fought in World War II for the rights of nations to independence and self-determination? What of its own history of expansion through war and conquest? It had waged a hundred-year war against the native Americans, driving them off their ancestral lands. The United States had instigated a war with Mexico and taken almost half its land, had sent marines at least twenty times into the countries of the Caribbean for power and profit, had seized Hawaii, had fought a brutal war to subjugate the Filipinos, and had sent 5,000 marines into Nicaragua in 1926. Our nation could hardly claim it believed in the right of self-determination unless it believed in it selectively.

Indeed, the United States had observed Fascist expansion without any strong reactions. When Italy invaded Ethiopia, the United States, while declaring an embargo on munitions, allowed American businesses to send oil to Italy, which was crucial for carrying on the war against Ethiopia. An official of the U.S. State Department, James E. Miller, reviewing a book on the relations between the United States and Mussolini, acknowledged that "American aid certainly reinforced the hold of fascism."

During the Spanish Civil War, while the Fascist side was receiving arms from Hitler and Mussolini, Roosevelt's administration sponsored a Neutrality Act that shut off help to the Spanish government fighting Franco.

Neither the invasion of Austria nor Czechoslovakia nor Poland brought the United States into armed collision with fascism. We went to war only when our possession Hawaii was attacked and when our navy was disabled by Japanese bombs. There was no reason to think that it was Japan's bombing of civilians at Pearl Harbor that caused us to declare war. Japan's attack on China in 1937, her massacre of civilians at Nanking, and her bombardments of helpless Chinese cities had not provoked the United States to war.

The sudden indignation against Japan contained a good deal of hypocrisy. The United States, along with Japan and the great European powers, had participated in the exploitation of China. Our Open Door Policy of 1901 accepted that ganging up of the great powers on China. The United States had exchanged notes with Japan in 1917 saying, "the Government of the United States recognizes that Japan has special interests in China," and in 1928, American consuls in China supported the coming of Japanese troops.

It was only when Japan threatened potential U.S. markets by its attempted takeover of China, but especially as it moved toward the tin, rubber, and oil of Southeast Asia, that the United States became alarmed and took those measures that led to the Japanese attack: a total embargo on scrap iron and a total embargo on oil in the summer of 1941.

A State Department memorandum on Japanese expansion, a year before Pearl Harbor, did not talk of the independence of China or the principle of self-determination. It said,

> Our general diplomatic and strategic position would be considerably weakened—by our loss of Chinese, Indian and South Seas markets (and by our loss of much of the Japanese market for our goods, as Japan would become more and more self-sufficient) as well as by insurmountable restrictions upon our access to the rubber, tin jute, and other vital materials of the Asian and Oceanic regions.

A War to Save the Jews

Did the United States enter the war because of its indignation at Hitler's treatment of the Jews? Hitler had been in power a year, and his campaign against the Jews had already begun when, in January 1934, a resolution was introduced into the Senate expressing "surprise and pain" at what the Germans were doing and asking for a restoration of Jewish rights. The State Department used its influence to get the resolution buried in committee.

Even after we were in the war against Germany (it should be noted that after Pearl Harbor Germany declared war on the United States, not vice versa) and reports began to arrive that Hitler was planning the annihilation of the Jews, Roosevelt's administration failed to take steps that might have saved thousands of lives.

Goebbels, minister of propaganda for Hitler's Germany, wrote in his diary on December 13, 1942: "At bottom, however, I believe both the

English and the Americans are happy we are exterminating the Jewish riffraff." Goebbels was undoubtedly engaging in wishful thinking, but in fact, the English and American governments had not shown by their actions that they were terribly concerned about the Jews. As for Roosevelt, he shunted the problem to the State Department, where it did not become a matter of high priority.

As an example of this failure to treat the situation as an emergency, Raul Hilberg, a leading scholar of the Holocaust, points to an event that took place in 1942. Early in August of that year, with 1,500,000 Jews already dead, the Jewish leader Stephen Wise was informed indirectly through a German industrialist that there was a plan in Hitler's headquarters for the extermination of all Jews; Wise brought the information to Under Secretary of State Sumner Welles. Welles asked him not to release the story until it was investigated for confirmation. Three months were spent checking the report. During that time a million Jews were killed in Europe.

It is doubtful that all those Jews could have been saved. But thousands could have been rescued. All the entrenched governments and organizations were negligent.

The British were slow and cautious. In March 1943, in the presence of Franklin D. Roosevelt, Secretary of State Hull pressed British Foreign Minister Anthony Eden on plans to rescue the 60,000 Jews in Bulgaria threatened with death. According to a memo by Roosevelt aide Harry Hopkins who was at that meeting, Eden worried that Polish and German Jews might then also ask to be rescued. "Hitler might well take us up on any such offer and there simply are not enough ships and means of transportation in the world to handle them." When there was a possibility of bombing the railroad lines leading into the murder chambers of Auschwitz, to stop further transportation of Jews there, the opportunity was ignored.

It should be noted that the Jewish organizations themselves behaved shamefully. In 1984, the American Jewish Commission on the Holocaust reviewed the historical record. It found that the American Jewish Joint Distribution Committee, a relief agency set up during World War II by the various Jewish groups, "was dominated by the wealthier and more

'American' elements of U.S. Jewry.... Thus, its policy was to do nothing in wartime that the U.S. government would not officially contenance."

Raul Hilberg points out that the Hungarian Jews might have been saved by a bargain: the Allies would not make air raids on Hungary if the Jews would be kept in the cities and not sent away. But "the Jews could not think in terms of interfering with the war effort, and the Allies on their part could not conceive of such a promise.... The Allied bombers roared over Hungary at will, killing Hungarians and Jews alike."

As I read this I recalled that one of the bombing raids I had done was on a town in Hungary.

Not only did waging war against Hitler fail to save the Jews, it may be that the war itself brought on the Final Solution of genocide. This is not to remove the responsibility from Hitler and the Nazis, but there is much evidence that Germany's anti-Semitic actions, cruel as they were, would not have turned to mass murder were it not for the psychic distortions of war, acting on already distorted minds. Hitler's early aim was forced emigration, not extermination, but the frenzy of it created an atmosphere in which the policy turned to genocide. This is the view of Princeton historian Arno Mayer, in his book *Why Did the Heavens Not Darken*, and it is supported by the chronology—that not until Germany was at war was the Final Solution adopted.

Hilberg, in his classic work on the Holocaust, says, "From 1938 to 1940, Hitler made extraordinary and unusual attempts to bring about a vast emigration scheme.... The Jews were not killed before the emigration policy was literally exhausted." The Nazis found that the Western powers were not anxious to cooperate in emigration and that no one wanted the Jews.

A War for Self-Determination?

We should examine another claim, that World War II was fought for the right of nations to determine their own destiny. This was declared with great fanfare by Winston Churchill and Franklin Roosevelt when they met off the coast of Newfoundland in August 1941 and announced the

Atlantic Charter, saying their countries, looking to the postwar world, respected "the right of all peoples to choose the form of government under which they will live." This was a direct appeal to the dependent countries of the world, especially the colonies of Britain, France, Holland, and Belgium, that their rights of self-determination would be upheld after the war. The support of the nonwhite colonial world was seen as crucial to the defeat of fascism.

However, two weeks before the Atlantic Charter, with the longtime French colony of Indochina very much in mind, acting Secretary of State Sumner Welles had given quiet assurances to the French: "This Government, mindful of its traditional friendship for France, has deeply sympathized with the desire of the French people to maintain their territories and to preserve them intact." And in late 1942, Roosevelt's personal representative told French General Henri Giraud, "It is thoroughly understood that French sovereignty will be reestablished as soon as possible throughout all the territory; metropolitan or colonial, over which flew the French flag in 1939." (These assurances of the United States are especially interesting in view of the claims of the United States during the Vietnam War, that the United States was fighting for the right of the Vietnamese to rule themselves.)

If neither saving the Jews nor guaranteeing the principle of self-determination was the war aim of the United States (and there is no evidence that either was the aim of Britain or the Soviet Union), then what *were* the principal motives? Overthrowing the governments of Hitler, Mussolini, and Tojo was certainly one of them. But was this desired on humanitarian grounds or because these regimes threatened the *positions* of the Allies in the world?

The rhetoric of morality—the language of freedom and democracy—had some substance to it, in that it represented the war aims of many ordinary citizens. However, it was not the citizenry but the governments who decided how the war was fought and who had the power to shape the world afterward.

Behind the halo of righteousness that surrounded the war against fascism, the usual motives of governments, repeatedly shown in history, were operating: the aggrandizement of the nation, more profit for its wealthy elite, and more power to its political leaders.

One of the most distinguished of British historians, A.J.P. Taylor, commented on World War II that "the British and American governments wanted no change in Europe except that Hitler should disappear." At the end of the war, novelist George Orwell, always conscious of class, wrote, "I see the railings [which enclosed the parks and had been torn up so the metal could be used in war production] are returning in one London park after another, so the lawful denizens of the squares can make use of their keys again, and the children of the poor can be kept out."

World War II was an opportunity for United States business to penetrate areas that up to that time had been dominated by England. Secretary of State Hull said early in the war,

> Leadership toward a new system of international relationships in trade and other economic affairs will devolve very largely upon the United States because of our great economic strength. We should assume this leadership, and the responsibility that goes with it, primarily for reasons of pure national self-interest.

Henry Luce, who owned three of the most influential magazines in the United States—*Life, Time*, and *Fortune*—and had powerful connections in Washington, wrote a famous editorial for *Life* in 1941 called "The American Century." This was the time, he said, "to accept wholeheartedly our duty and our opportunity as the most powerful and vital nation in the world and in consequence to exert upon the world the full impact of our influence, for such purposes as we see fit and by such means as we see fit."

The British, weakened by war, clearly could not maintain their old empire. In 1944 England and the United States signed a pact on oil agreeing on "the principle of equal opportunity." This meant the United States was muscling in on England's traditional domination of Middle East oil. A study of the international oil business by the English writer Anthony Sampson concluded,

By the end of the war the dominant influence in Saudi Arabia was unquestionably the United States. King Ibn Saud was regarded no longer as a wild desert warrior, but as a key piece in the power-game, to be wooed by the West. Roosevelt, on his way back from Yalta in February, 1945, entertained the King on the cruiser Quincy, together with his entourage of fifty, including two sons, a prime minister, an astrologer and flocks of sheep for slaughter.

There was a critic inside the American government, not a politician but poet Archibald MacLeish, who briefly served as assistant secretary of state. He worried about the postwar world: "As things are now going the peace we will make, the peace we seem to be making, will be a peace of oil, a peace of gold, a peace of shipping, a peace, in brief..without moral purpose or human interest."

A War Against Racism?

If the war was truly a war of moral purpose, against the Nazi idea of superior and inferior races, then we might have seen action by the U.S. government to eliminate racial segregation. Such segregation had been declared lawful by the Supreme Court in 1896 and existed in both South and North, accepted by both state and national governments.

The armed forces were segregated by race. When I was in basic training at Jefferson Barracks, Missouri, in 1943, it did not occur to me, so typical an American white was I, that there were no black men in training with us. But it was a huge base, and one day, taking a long walk to the other end of it, I was suddenly aware that all the GIs around me were black. There was a squad of blacks taking a ten-minute break from hiking in the sun, lying on a small grassy incline, and singing a hymn that surprised me at the moment, but that I realized later was quite appropriate to their situation: "Ain't Gonna Study War No More."

My air crew sailed to England on the Queen Mary. That elegant passenger liner had been converted into a troop ship. There were 16,000 men aboard, and 4,000 of them were black. The whites had quarters on deck and just below deck. The blacks were housed separately, deep in the hold of the ship, around the engine room, in the darkest, dirtiest sections. Meals were taken in four shifts (except for the officers, who ate in prewar *Queen Mary* style in a chandeliered ballroom—the war was not being fought to disturb class privilege), and the blacks had to wait until three shifts of whites had finished eating.

On the home front, racial discrimination in employment continued, and it was not until A. Philip Randolph, head of the Brotherhood of Sleeping Car Porters, a union of black workers, threatened to organize a march on Washington during the war and embarrass the Roosevelt administration before the world that the president signed an order setting up a Fair Employment Practices Commission. But its orders were not enforced and job discrimination continued. A spokesman for a West Coast aviation plant said, "The Negro will be considered only as janitors and in other similar capacities.... Regardless of their training as aircraft workers, we will not employ them."

There was no organized black opposition to the war, but there were many signs of bitterness at the hypocrisy of a war against fascism that did nothing about American racism. One black journalist wrote: "The Negro...is angry, resentful, and utterly apathetic about the war. 'Fight for what?' he is asking. 'This war doesn't mean a thing to me. If we win I lose, so what?'"

A student at a black college told his teacher: "The Army jim-crows us. The Navy lets us serve only as messmen. The Red Cross refuses our blood. Employers and labor unions shut us out. Lynchings continue. We are disenfranchised, jim-crowed, spat upon. What more could Hitler do than that?" That student's statement was repeated by Walter White, a leader of the National Association for the Advancement of Colored People (NAACP), to an audience of several thousand black people in the Midwest, expecting that they would disapprove. Instead, as he recalled, "To my surprise and dismay the audience burst into such applause that it took me some thirty or forty seconds to quiet it."

In January 1943, there appeared in a Negro newspaper a "Draftee's Prayer":

Dear Lord, today
I go to war:
To fight, to die.
Tell me, what for?
Dear Lord, I'll fight,
I do not fear,
Germans or Japs
My fears are here
America!

In one little-known incident of World War II, two transport ships being loaded with ammunition by U.S. sailors at the Port Chicago naval base in California suddenly blew up on the night of July 17, 1944. It was an enormous explosion, and its glare could be seen in San Francisco, thirty-five miles away. More than 300 sailors were killed, two-thirds of them black, because blacks were given the hard jobs of ammunition loaders. "It was the worst home front disaster of World War II," historian Robert Allen writes in his book *The Port Chicago Mutiny*.

Three weeks later 328 of the survivors were asked to load ammunition again; 258 of them refused, citing unsafe conditions. They were immediately jailed. Fifty of them were then court-martialed on a charge of mutiny, and received sentences ranging from eight to fifteen years imprisonment. It took a massive campaign by the NAACP and its counsel, Thurgood Marshall, to get the sentences reduced.

To the Japanese who lived on the West Coast of the United States, it quickly became clear that the war against Hitler was not accompanied by a spirit of racial equality. After the attack by Japan on Pearl Harbor, anger rose against all people of Japanese ancestry. One Congressman said, "I'm for catching every Japanese in America, Alaska and Hawaii now and putting them in concentration camps.... Damn them! Let's get rid of them now!"

Hysteria grew. Roosevelt, persuaded by racists in the military that the Japanese on the West Coast constituted a threat to the security of the country, signed Executive Order 9066 in February 1942. This empowered the army, without warrants or indictments or hearings, to arrest every Japanese-American on the West Coast—110,000 men, women and children—to take them from their homes, to transport them to camps far in the interior, and to keep them there under prison conditions.

Three-fourths of the Japanese so removed from their homes were Nisei—children born in the United States of Japanese parents and, therefore American citizens. The other fourth—the Issei, born in Japan—were barred by law from becoming citizens. In 1944 the United States Supreme Court upheld the forced evacuation on the grounds of military necesssity.

Data uncovered in the 1980s by legal historian Peter Irons showed that the army falsified material in its brief to the Supreme Court. When Congress in 1983 was considering financial compensation to the Japanese who had been removed from their homes and lost their possessions during the war, John J. McCloy wrote an article in *The New York Times* opposing such compensation, defending the action as necessary. As Peter Irons discovered in his research, it was McCloy, then assistant secretary of war, who had ordered the deletion of a critical footnote in the Justice Department brief to the Supreme Court, a footnote that cast great doubt on the army's assertions that the Japanese living on the West Coast were a threat to American security.

Michi Weglyn was a young girl when her family experienced evacuation and detention. She tells in her book *Years of Infamy* of bungling in the evacuation; of misery, confusion, and anger; but also of Japanese-American dignity and of fighting back. There were strikes, petitions, mass meetings, refusals to sign loyalty oaths, and riots against the camp authorities.

Only a few Americans protested publicly. The press often helped to feed racism. Reporting the bloody battle of Iwo Jima in the Pacific, *Time* magazine said, "The ordinary unreasoning Jap is ignorant. Perhaps he is human. Nothing..indicates it."

In the 1970s, Peter Ota, then fifty-seven, was interviewed by Studs Terkel. His parents had come from Japan in 1904, and became respected members of the Los Angeles community. Ota was born in the United States. He remembered what had happened in the war:

On the evening of December 7, 1941, my father was at a wedding. He was dressed in a tuxedo. When the reception was over, the FBI agents were waiting. They rounded up at least a dozen wedding guests and took 'em to county jail.

For a few days we didn't know what happened. We heard nothing. When we found out, my mother, my sister and myself went to jail.. When my father walked through the door my mother was so humiliated.... She cried. He was in prisoner's clothing, with a denim jacket and a number on the back. The shame and humiliation just broke her down.... Right after that day she got very ill and contracted tuberculosis. She had to be sent to a sanitarium.... She was there till she died....

My father was transferred to Missoula, Montana. We got letters from him—censored, of course.... It was just my sister and myself. I was fifteen, she was twelve.... School in camp was a joke.... One of our basic subjects was American history. They talked about freedom all the time. (Laughs.)

In England there was similar hysteria. People with German-sounding names were picked up and interned. In the panic, a number of Jewish refugees who had German names were arrested and thrown into the same camps. There were thousands of Italians who were living in England, and when Italy entered World War II in June of 1940, Winston Churchill gave the order: "Collar the lot." Italians were picked up and interned, the windows of Italian shops and restaurants were smashed by patriotic mobs. A British ship carrying Italian internees to Canada was sunk by a German submarine and everyone drowned.

A War for Democracy?

It was supposed to be a war for freedom. But in the United States, when Trotskyists and members of the Socialist Workers Party spoke out in criticism of the war, eighteen of them were prosecuted in 1943 in Minneapolis. The Smith Act, passed in 1940, extended the anti-free-speech provisions of the World War I Espionage Act to peacetime. It prohibited joining any group or publishing any material that advocated revolution or that might lead to refusal of military service. The Trotskyists were sentenced to prison terms, and the Supreme Court refused to review their case.

Fortunes were made during the war, and wealth was concentrated in fewer and fewer hands. By 1941 three-fourths of the value of military contracts were handled by fifty-six large corporations. Pressure was put on the labor unions to pledge they would not strike. But they saw their wages frozen, and profits of corporations rising, and so strikes went on. There were 14,000 strikes during the war, involving over 6 million workers, more than in any comparable period in American history.

An insight into what great profits were made during the war came years later, when the mulitmillionaire John McCone was nominted by President John F. Kennedy to head the CIA. The Sentate Armed Services Committee, considering the nomination, was informed that in World War II, McCone and associates in a shipbuilding company had made $44 million on an investment of $100,000. Reacting indignantly to criticism of McCone, one of his supporters on the Senate committee asked him:

> Sen. Symington: Now, it is still legal in America, if not to make a profit, at least to try to make a profit, is it not?
> McCone: That is my understanding.

Bruce Catton, a writer and historian working in Washington during the war, commented bitingly on the retention of wealth and power in the same hands, despite a war that seemed to promise a new world of social reform. He wrote:

> We were committed to a defeat of the Axis but to nothing else.... It was solemnly decided that the war effort must not be used to bring about social or economic reform and to him that hath shall be given....
> And through it all...the people were not trusted with the facts or relied on to display that intelligence, sanity, and innate decency of spirit, upon which democracy...finally rests. In a very real sense, our government spent the war years looking desperately for some safe middle ground between Hitler and Abraham Lincoln.

Dresden and Hiroshima

It becomes difficult to sustain the claim that a war is just when both sides commit atrocities, unless one wants to argue that their atrocities are worse than ours. True, nothing done by the Allied Powers in World War II matches in utter viciousness the deliberate gassing, shooting, and burning of six million Jews and four million others by the Nazis. The deaths caused by the Allies were less, but still so massive as to throw doubt on the justice of a war that includes such acts.

Early in the war, various world leaders condemned the indescriminate bombing of city populations. Italy had bombed civilians in Ethiopia; Japan, in China; Germany and Italy, in the Spanish Civil War. Germany had dropped bombs on Rotterdam in Holland, on Coventry in England, and other places. Roosevelt described these bombings as "inhuman barbarism that has profoundly shocked the conscience of humanity."

But very soon, the United States and Britain were doing the same thing and on a far larger scale. When the Allied leaders met at Casablanca in January 1943, they agreed on massive air attacks to achieve "the destruction and dislocation of the German military, industrial and economic system and the undermining of the morale of the German people to the point where their capacity for armed resistance is fatally weakened." Churchill and his advisers had decided that bombing working-class districts of German cities would accomplish just that, "the undermining of the morale of the German people."

The saturation bombing of the German cities began. There were raids of a thousand planes on Cologne, Essen, Frankfurt, and Hamburg.

The British flew at night and did "area bombing" with no pretense of aiming at specific military targets.

The Americans flew in the daytime, pretending to precision, but bombing from high altitudes made that impossible. When I was doing my practice bombing in Deming, New Mexico, before going overseas, our egos were built up by having us fly at 4,000 feet and drop a bomb within twenty feet of the target. But at 11,000 feet, we were more likely to be 200 feet away. And when we flew combat missions, we did it from 30,000 feet, and might miss by a quarter of a mile. Hardly "precision bombing."

There was huge self-deception. We had been angered when the Germans bombed cities and killed several hundred or a thousand people. But now the British and Americans were killing tens of thousands in a single air strike. Michael Sherry, in his study of aerial bombing, notes that "so few in the air force asked questions." Sherry says there was no clear thinking about the effects of the bombing. Some generals objected, but were overruled by civilians. The technology crowded out moral considerations. Once the planes existed, targets had to be found.

It was terror bombing, and the German city of Dresden was the extreme example. (The city and the event are immortalized in fiction by Kurt Vonnegut's comic, bitter novel, *Slaughterhouse Five*.) It was February, 1945, the Red Army was eighty miles to the east and it was clear that Germany was on the way to defeat. In one day and one night of bombing, by American and British planes, the tremendous heat generated by the bombs created a vacuum, and an enomous firestorm swept the city, which was full of refugees at the time, increasing the population to a million. More than 100,000 people died.

The British pilot of a Lancaster bomber recalled, "There was a sea of fire covering in my estimation some forty square miles. We were so aghast at the awesome blaze that although alone over the city, we flew around in a stand-off position for many minutes before turning for home, quite subdued by our imagination of the horror that must be below."

One incident remembered by survivors is that on the afternoon of February 14, 1945, American fighter planes machine-gunned clusters of refugees on the banks of the Elbe. A German woman told of this years later: "We ran along the Elbe stepping over the bodies."

Winston Churchill, who seemed to have no moral qualms about his policy of indiscriminate bombing, described the annihilation of Dresden in his wartime memoirs with a simple statement: "We made a heavy raid in the latter month on Dresden, then a centre of communication of Germany's Eastern Front."

At one point in the war Churchill ordered thousands of anthrax bombs from a plant that was secretly producing them in the United States. His chief science adviser, Lord Cherwell, had informed him in February 1944: "Any animal breathing in minute quantities of these N (anthrax) spores is extremely likely to die suddenly but peacefully within the week. There is no known cure and no effective prophylaxis. There is little doubt that it is equally lethal to human beings." He told Churchill that a half dozen bombers could carry enough four-pound anthrax bombs to kill everyone within a square mile. However, production delays got in the way of this plan.

The actor Richard Burton once wrote an article for *The New York Times* about his experience playing the role of Winston Churchill in a television drama:

> In the course of preparing myself...I realized afresh that I hate Churchill and all of his kind. I hate them virulently. They have stalked down the corridors of endless power all through history.... What man of sanity would say on hearing of the atrocities committed by the Japanese against British and Anzac prisoners of war, "We shall wipe them out, everyone of them, men, women, and children. There shall not be a Japanese left on the face of the earth"? Such simple-minded cravings for revenge leave me with a horrified but reluctant awe for such single-minded and merciless ferocity.

When Burton's statement appeared in the "Arts and Leisure" section of *The New York Times*, he was banned from future BBC productions. The supervisor of drama productions for BBC said, "As far as I am concerned, he will never work for us again.. Burton acted in an unprofessional way."

It seems that however moral is the cause that initiates a war (in the minds of the public, in the mouths of the politicians), it is in the nature of war to corrupt that morality until the rule becomes "An eye for an eye, a tooth for a tooth," and soon it is not a matter of equivalence, but indescriminate revenge.

The policy of saturation bombing became even more brutal when B29s, with carried twice the bombload as the planes we flew in Europe, attacked Japanese cities with incendiaries, turning them into infernos.

In one raid on Tokyo, after midnight on March 10, 1945, 300 B29s left the city in flames, fanned by a strong northwest wind. The fires could be seen by pilots 150 miles out in the Pacific Ocean. A million people were left homeless. It is estimated that 100,000 people died that night. Many of them attempting to escape leaped into the Sumida River and drowned. A Japanese novelist who was twelve years old at the time, described the scene years later: "The fire was like a living thing. It ran, just like a creature, chasing us."

By the time the atomic bomb was dropped on Hiroshima (August 6, 1945) and another on Nagasaki (three days later), the moral line had been crossed psychologically by the massive bombings in Europe and by the fire bombings of Tokyo and other cities.

The bomb on Hiroshima left perhaps 140,000 dead; the one on Nagasaki, 70,000 dead. Another 130,000 died in the next five years. Hundreds of thousands of others were left radiated and maimed. These numbers are based on the most detailed report that exists on the effects of the bombings; it was compiled by thirty-four Japanese specialists and was published in 1981.

The deception and self-deception that accompanied these atrocities was remarkable. Truman told the public, "The world will note that the first atomic bomb was dropped on Hiroshima, a military base. That was because we wished in this first attack to avoid, insofar as possible, the killing of civilians."

Even the possibility that American prisoners of war would be killed in these bombings did not have any effect on the plans. On July 31, nine days before Nagasaki was bombed, the headquarters of the U.S. Army Strategic Air Forces on Guam (the take-off airfield for the atomic bombings) sent a message to the War Department:

Reports prisoner of war sources not verified by photo give location of Allied prisoner-of-war camp, one mile north of center of city of Nagasaki. Does this influence the choice of this target for initial Centerboard operation? Request immediate reply.

The reply came, "Targets previously assigned for Centerboard remain unchanged."

The terrible momentum of war continued even after the bombings of Hiroshima and Nagasaki. The end of the war was a few days away, yet B29s continued their missions. On August 14, five days after the Nagasaki bombing and the day before the actual acceptance of surrender terms, 449 B29s went out from the Marianas for a daylight strike and 372 more went out that night. Altogether, more than 1,000 planes were sent to bomb Japanese cities. There were no American losses. The last plane had not yet returned when Truman announced the Japanese had surrendered.

Japanese writer Oda Makoto describes that August 14 in Osaka, where he lived. He was a boy. He went out into the streets and found in the midst of the corpses American leaflets written in Japanese, which had been dropped with the bombs: Your government has surrendered; the war is over."

The American public, already conditioned to massive bombing, accepted the atomic bombings with equanimity, indeed with joy. I remember my own reaction. When the war ended in Europe, my crew flew our plane back to the United States. We were given a thirty-day furlough and then had to report for duty to be sent to Japan to continue bombing. My wife and I decided to spend that time in the countryside. Waiting for the bus to take us, I picked up the morning newspaper, August 7, 1945. The headline was "Atomic Bomb Dropped on Hiroshima." My immediate reaction was elation: "The war will end. I won't have to go to the Pacific."

I had no idea what the explosion of the atomic bomb had done to the men, women, and children of Hiroshima. It was abstract and distant, as were the deaths of the people from the bombs I had dropped in Europe from a height of six miles; I was unable to see anything below, there was no visible blood, and there were no audible screams. And I knew nothing of the imminence of a Japanese surrender. It was only later when I read John Hersey's *Hiroshima*, when I read the testimony of Japanese survivors, and when I studied the history of the decision to drop the bomb that I was outraged by what had been done.

It seems that once an initial judgment has been made that a war is just, there is a tendency to stop thinking, to assume then that everything done on behalf of victory is morally acceptable. I had myself participated in the bombing of cities, without even considering whether there was any relationship between what I was doing and the elimination of fascism in the world. Thus a war that apparently begins with a "good" cause—stopping aggression, helping victims, or punishing brutality—ends with its own aggression, creates more victims than before, and brings out more brutality than before, on both sides. The Holocaust, a plan made and executed in the ferocious atmosphere of war, and the saturation bombings, also created in the frenzy of war, are evidence of this.

The good cause in World War II was the defeat of fascism. And, in fact, it ended with that defeat: the corpse of Mussolini hanging in the public square in Milan; Hitler burned to death in his underground bunker; Tojo, captured and sentenced to death by an international tribunal. But forty million people were dead, and the elements of fascism—militarism, racism, imperialism, dictatorship, ferocious nationalism, and war—were still at large in the postwar world.

Two of those forty million were my closest Air Force friends, Joe Perry and Ed Plotkin. We had suffered through basic training and rode horses and flew Piper Cubs in Burlington, Vermont, and played basketball at Santa Ana before going our own ways to different combat zones. Both were killed in the final weeks of the war. For years afterward, they appeared in my dreams. In my waking hours, the question grew: What did they really die for?

We were victorious over fascism, but this left two superpowers dominating the world, vying for control of other nations, carving out new spheres of influence, on a scale even larger than that attempted by the Fascist powers. Both superpowers supported dictatorships all over the world: the Soviet Union in Eastern Europe and the United States in Latin America, Korea, and the Philippines.

The war machines of the Axis powers were destroyed, but the Soviet Union and the United States were bulding military machines greater than the world had ever seen, piling up frightful numbers of nuclear weapons, soon equivalent to a million Hiroshima-type bombs. They were preparing for a war to keep the peace, they said (this had also been said before World War I) but those preparations were such that if war took place (by accident? by miscalculation?) it would make the Holocaust look puny.

Hitler's aggression was over but wars continued, which the superpowers either initiated or fed with military aid or observed without attempting to halt them. Two million people died in Korea; two to five million in Vietnam, Cambodia, and Laos; one million in Indonesia; perhaps two million in the Nigerian civil war; one million in the Iran-Iraq War; and many more in Latin America, Africa, and the Middle East. It is estimated that, in the forty years after 1945, there were 150 wars, with twenty million casualties.

The victorious and morally righteous superpowers stood by in the postwar world while millions—more than had died in Hitler's Holocaust—starved to death. They made gestures, but allowed national ambitions and interpower rivalries to stand in the way of saving the hungry. A United Nations official reported, with great bitterness that

> in pursuit of political objectives in the Nigerian Civil War, a number of great and small nations, including Britain and the United States, worked to prevent supplies of food and medicine from reaching the starving children of rebel Biafra.

Swept up in the obvious rightness of a crusade to rid the world of fascism, most people supported or participated in that crusade, to the point of risking their lives. But there were skeptics, especially among the nonwhite peoples of the world—blacks in the United States and the colonized millions of the British Empire (Gandhi withheld his support).

The extraordinary black writer Zora Neale Hurston wrote her memoir, *Dust Tracks on a Road*, at the start of World War II. Just before it was to come out, the Japanese attacked Pearl Harbor, and her publisher,

Lippincott, removed a section of the book in which she wrote bitterly about the "democracies" of the West and their hypocrisy. She said:

> All around me, bitter tears are being shed over the fate of Holland, Belgium, France and England. I must confess to being a little dry around the eyes. I hear people shaking with shudders at the thought of Germany collecting taxes in Holland. I have not heard a word against Holland collecting one twelfth of poor people's wages in Asia. Hitler's crime is that he is actually doing a thing like that to his own kind....
>
> As I see it, the doctrines of democracy deal with the aspirations of men's souls, but the application deals with things. One hand in somebody else's pocket and one on your gun, and you are highly civilized.... Desire enough for your own use only, and you are a heathen. Civilized people have things to show to their neighbors.

The editor at Lippincott wrote on her manuscript, "Suggest eliminating international opinions as irrelevant to autobiography." Only when the book was reissued in 1984 did the censored passages appear.

Hurston, in a letter she wrote to a journalist friend in 1946, showed her indignation at the hypocrisy that accompanied the war:

> I am amazed at the complacency of Negro press and public. Truman is a monster. I can think of him as nothing else but the Butcher of Asia. Of his grin of triumph on giving the order to drop the Atom bombs on Japan. Of his maintaining troops in China who are shooting the starving Chinese for stealing a handful of food.

Some white writers were resistant to the fanaticism of war. After it was over, Joseph Heller wrote his biting, brilliant satire *Catch-22* and Kurt Vonnegut wrote *Slaughterhouse Five*. In the 1957 film *Bridge on the River Kwai*, the Japanese military is obsessed with building a bridge, and the British are obsessed with destroying it. At the end it is blown up and a British lieutenant, barely surviving, looks around at the river strewn with corpses and mutters: "Madness. Madness."

There were pacifists in the United States who went to prison rather than participate in World War II. There were 350,000 draft evaders in the United States. Six thousand men went to prison as conscientious objectors; one out of every six inmates in U.S. federal prisons was a conscientious objector to the war.

But the general mood in the United States was support. Liberals, conservatives, and Communists agreed that it was a just war. Only a few voices were raised publicly in Europe and the United States to question the motives of the participants, the means by which the war was being conducted, and the ends that would be achieved. Very few tried to stand back from the battle and take a long view. One was the French worker-philosopher Simone Weil. Early in 1945 she wrote in a new magazine called *Politics:*

> Whether the mask is labelled Fascism, Democracy, or Dictatorship or the Proletariat, our great adversary remains the Apparatus—the bureaucracy, the police, the military.... No matter what the circumstances, the worst betrayal will always be to subordinate ourselves to this Apparatus, and to trample underfoot, in its service, all human values in ourselves and in others.

The editor of *Politics* was an extraordinary American intellectual named Dwight MacDonald, who with his wife, Nancy, produced the magazine as an outlet for unorthodox points of view. After the bombing of Hiroshima, MacDonald refused to join in the general jubilation. He wrote with a fury:

> The CONCEPTS "WAR" AND "PROGRESS" ARE NOW OBSO-LETE...THE FUTILITY OF MODERN WARFARE SHOULD NOW BE CLEAR. Must we not now conclude, with Simone Weil, that the technical aspect of war today is the evil, regardless of political factors? Can one imagine that the atomic bomb could ever be used "in a good cause"?

But what was the alternative to war, with Germany on the march in Europe, Japan on its rampage through Asia, and Italy looking for empire? This is the toughest possible question. Once the history of an epoch has run its course, it is very difficult to imagine an alternate set of events, to imagine that some act or acts might set in motion a whole new train of circumstances, leading in a different direction.

Would it have been possible to trade time and territory for human life? Was there an alternative preferable to using the most modern weapons of destruction for mass annihilation? Can we try to imagine instead of a six-year war a ten-year or twenty-year period of resistance; of guerilla warfare, strikes, and noncooperation; of underground movements, sabotage, and paralysis of vital communication and transportation; and of clandestine propaganda for the organization of a larger and larger opposition?

Even in the midst of war, some nations occupied by the Nazis were able to resist: the Danes, the Norweigians, and the Bulgarians refused to give up their Jews. Gene Sharp, on the basis of his study of resistance movements in World War II, writes:

> During the second World War—in such occupied countries as the Netherlands, Norway and Denmark—patriots resisted their Nazi overlords and internal puppets by such weapons as underground newspapers, labor slowdowns, general strikes, refusal of collaboration, special boycotts of German troops and quislings, and noncooperation with fascist controls and efforts to restructure their societies' institutions.

Guerrilla warfare is more selective, its violence more limited and more discriminate, than conventional war. It is less centralized and more democratic by nature, requiring the commitment, the initiative, and the cooperation of ordinary people who do not need to be conscripted, but who are motivated by their desire for freedom and justice.

History is full of instances of successful resistance (although we are not informed very much about this) without violence and against tyranny, by people using strikes, boycotts, propaganda, and a dozen different ingenious forms of struggle. Gene Sharp, in his book *The Politics of Non-Violent Action*, records hundreds of instances and dozens of methods of action.

Since the end of World War II, we have seen dictatorships overthrown by mass movements that mobilized so much popular oppostion that the tyrant finally had to flee in Iran, in Nicaragua, in the Philippines, and in Haiti. Granted, the Nazi machine was formidable, efficient, and ruthless.

202 / HOWARD ZINN ON WAR

But there are limits to conquest. A point is reached where the conquerer has swallowed too much territory, has to control too many people. Great empires have fallen when it was thought they would last forever.

We have seen, in the Eighties, mass movements of protest arise in the tightly controlled Communist countries of Eastern Europe, forcing dramatic changes in Hungary, Czechoslovakia, Poland, Bulgaria, Rumania, and East Germnay. The Spanish people, having lost a million lives in their civil war, waited out Franco. He died, as all men do, and the dictatorship was over. For Portugal, the resistance in its outlying African Empire weakened control; corruption grew and the long dictatorship of Salazar was overthrown—without a bloodbath.

There is a fable written by German playwright Bertolt Brecht that goes roughly like this: A man living alone answers a knock at the door. When he opens it, he sees in the doorway the powerful body, the cruel face, of The Tyrant. The Tyrant asks, "Will you submit?" The man does not reply. He steps aside. The Tyrant enters and establishes himself in the man's house. The man serves him for years. Then The Tyrant becomes sick from food poisoning. He dies. The man wraps the body, opens the door, gets rids of the body, comes back to his house, closes the door behind him, and says, firmly, "No."

Violence is not the only form of power. Sometimes it is the least effective. Always it is the most vicious, for the perpetrator as well as for the victim. And it is corrupting.

Immediately after the war, Albert Camus, the great French writer who fought in the underground against the Nazis, wrote in *Combat*, the daily newspaper of the French Resistance. In his essay called "Neither Victims Nor Executioners," he considered the tens of millions of dead caused by the war and asked that the world reconsider fanaticism and violence:

> All I ask is that, in the midst of a murderous world, we agree to reflect on murder and to make a choice.... Over the expanse of five continents throughout the comng years an endless struggle is going to be pursued between violence and friendly persuasion, a struggle in which, granted, the

former has a thousand times the chances of success than has the latter. But I have always held that, if he who bases his hopes on human nature is a fool, he who gives up in the face of circumstances is a coward. And henceforth, the only honorable course will be to stake everything on a formidable gamble: that words are more powerful than munitions.

Whatever alternative scenarios we can imagine to replace World War II and its mountain of corpses, it really doesn't matter any more. That war is over. The practical effect of declaring World War II just is not for that war, but for the wars that follow. And that effect has been a dangerous one, because the glow of rightness that accompanied that war has been transferred, by false analogy and emotional carryover, to other wars. To put it another way, perhaps the worst consequence of World War II is that it kept alive the idea that war could be just.

Looking at World War II in perspective, looking at the world it created and the terror that grips our century, should we not bury for all time the idea of just war?

Some of the participants in that "good war" had second thoughts. Former GI Tommy Bridges, who after the war became a policeman in Michigan, expressed his feelings to Studs Terkel:

> It was a useless war, as every war is.... How gaddamn foolish it is, the war. They's no war in the world that's worth fighting for, I don't care where it is. They can't tell me any different. Money, money is the thing that causes it all. I wouldn't be a bit surprised that the people that start wars and promote 'em are the men that make the money, make the ammunition, make the clothing and so forth. Just think of the poor kids that are starvin' to death in Asia and so forth that could be fed with how much you make one big shell out of.

Higher up in the military ranks was Admiral Gene LaRocque, who also spoke to Studs Terkel about the war:

> I had been in thirteen battle engagements, had sunk a submarine, and was the first man ashore in the landing at Roi. In that four years, I thought, What a hell of a waste of a man's life. I lost a lot of friends. I had the task of telling my roommate's parents about our last days together. You lose

204 / HOWARD ZINN ON WAR

limbs, sight, part of your life—for what? Old men send young men to war. Flag, banners, and patriotic sayings..

We've institutionalized militarism. This came out of World War Two.... It gave us the National Security Council. It gave us the CIA, that is able to spy on you and me this very moment. For the first time in the history of man, a country has divided up the world into military districts.... You could argue World War Two had to be fought. Hitler had to be stopped. Unfortunately, we translate it unchanged to the situation today....

I hate it when they say, "He gave his life for his country." Nobody gives their life for anything. We steal the lives of these kids. We take it away from them. They don't die for the honor and glory of their country. We kill them.

Granted that we have started in this century with the notion of just war, we don't have to keep it. Perhaps the change in our thinking can be as dramatic, as clear, as that in the life of a French general, whose obituary in 1986 was headed: "Gen. Jacques Paris de Bollardiere, War Hero Who Became a Pacifist, Dead at the age of 78."

He had served in the Free French Forces in Africa during World War II, later parachuted into France and Holland to organize the Resistance, and commanded an airborne unit in Indochina from 1946 to 1953. But in 1957, according to the obituary, he "caused an uproar in the French army when he asked to be relieved of his command in Algeria to protest the torture of Algerian rebels. In 1961 he began to speak out against militarism and nuclear weapons. He created an organization called The Alternative Movement for Non-Violence and in 1973 participated in a protest expedition to France's South Pacific nuclear testing site.

It remains to be seen how many people in our time will make that journey from war to nonviolent action against war. It is the great challenge or our time: How to achieve justice, with struggle, but without war.

Suggestions for Further Reading

Some suggestions for further reading on war. I am not giving a formal listing of publishers, dates, and places because public libraries can easily locate books by title and/or author.

The first blow to my youthful awe of martial heroism came when I was eighteen or so and read Walter Millis' *The Road to War*, a devastating critique of our nation's entrance into World War I. But probably the most powerful influences that, for me, turned the glamour of war into unmitigated horror were novels: Henry Barbusse's *Under Fire*, Erich Maria Remarque's *All Quiet on the Western Front*, and even more, Dalton Trumbo's *Johnny Got His Gun*, all part of the revulsion that came after the first World War.

Despite my enthusiastic participation in World War II as an Air Force bombardier, it did not take long after the war to begin to reconsider the question of whether any war, even that "best of wars" (as I termed it, ironically, in one of my essays later) was justified. Probably the first piece of writing that turned me in that direction was John Hersey's *Hiroshima*. Later, the novels *Catch-22* by Joseph Heller, and *Slaughterhouse Five* by Kurt Vonnegut, fit perfectly into my now-cynical view of that war.

My studies and teaching in American history, giving me a close look at U.S. foreign policy, persuaded me that our military interventions at U.S. foreign policy, persuaded me that our military interventions abroad, in Latin America, in the Pacific, were part of the empire-building among the Western nations, for reasons of political power and corporate profit. William Appleman Williams' *The Tragedy of American Diplomacy*, was an early influence. For books on Vietnam, I would recommend Marilyn Young's vibrant, powerful history, *The Vietnam Wars*. On U.S. foreign policy since the inception of the cold war, there is no better guide than the writings of Noam Chomsky. I will just mention a few of his books: *Necessary Illusions*, *Deterring Democracy*, and *Manufacturing Consent* (the latter written with Edward Herman).

For alternatives to war, there are a number of books by Gene Sharp, especially *The Politics of Non-Violent Direct Action*.

Also by Howard Zinn:

LaGuardia in Congress (Cornell University Press, 1959)

The Southern Mystique (Alfred Knopf, 1964)

SNCC: The New Abolitionists (Beacon Press, 1964)

New Deal Thought, ed. (Bobbs Merrill, 1965)

Vietnam: The Logic of Withdrawal (Beacon Press, 1967)

Disobedience and Democracy (Random House, 1968)

The Politics of History (Beacon Press, 1970)

The Pentagon Papers: Critical Essays, ed. with Noam Chomsky (Beacon Press, 1972)

Postwar America (Bobbs Merrill, 1973)

Justice in Everyday Life, ed. (William Morrow, 1974)

A People's History of the United States (Harper & Row, 1980)

The Twentieth Century: A People's History (HarperCollins, 1984)

Declarations of Independence: Cross-Examining American Ideology (HarperCollins, 1990)

Failure to Quit: Reflections of an Optimistic Historian (Common Courage Press, 1993)

You Can't Be Neutral on a Moving Train (Beacon Press, 1994)

The Zinn Reader (Seven Stories, 1997)

Howard Zinn on History (Seven Stories, 2001)

HOWARD ZINN grew up in the immigrant slums of Brooklyn, where he worked in shipyards in his late teens. He saw combat duty as an air force bombardier in World War II, and afterward received his doctorate in history from Columbia University. His first book, *La Guardia in Congress,* was an Albert Berveridge Prize winner. In 1956, he moved with his wife and children to Atlanta to become chairman of the history department of Spelman College. He has since written and edited many more books, including *A People's History of the United States; SNCC: The New Abolitionist; Disobedience and Democracy; The Politics of History; The Pentagon Papers: Critical Essays; You Can't Be Neutral on a Moving Train: A Personal History of Our Times;* and *The Zinn Reader.*

Zinn is also the author of three plays: *Emma, Daughter of Venus,* and *Marx in Soho.* Among the many honors Zinn has received, the most recent is the 1998 Lannan Literary Award for nonfiction. A professor emeritus of political science at Boston University, he lives with his wife, Roslyn, in the Boston area, near their children and grandchildren.